S0-BSE-753

# Choose To Believe

## A Practical Guide To Living Your Dreams

# Alan Tutt

### Author of:

Harmonic Prayer: How to Instantly Increase Your Prayer Power
Awaken the Avatar Within
28 Days to Effortless Success
Prosperity From the Inside Out
Treasure Map to Online Riches
Keys To Power Persuasion

### Creator of:

EmBRACES Belief Entrainment System

**PowerKeys Publishing**
Grand Rapids, MI
www.PowerKeysPub.com

## LEGAL DISCLAIMER

Neither the publisher nor the author are engaged in dispensing medical advice or prescribing the use of any technique as a form of treatment for physical, emotional, or medical problems without the advice of a physician, either directly or indirectly. In the event you use any of the information in this book for yourself, which is your constitutional right, the author and publisher assume no responsibility for your actions. If you do not agree to be bound by these terms, please return the book for a refund.

# Choose To Believe

## A Practical Guide To
## Living Your Dreams

## Alan Tutt

**PowerKeys Publishing**
Grand Rapids, MI
www.PowerKeysPub.com

**Publisher's Cataloging-in-Publication**
*(Provided by Quality Books, Inc.)*

Tutt, Alan.
  Choose to believe : a practical guide to living your
dreams / Alan Tutt. -- 1st ed.
  p. cm.
  Includes bibliographical references and index.
  ISBN-13: 978-0-9796726-4-4
  ISBN-10: 0-9796726-4-3
  ISBN-13: 978-0-9796726-3-7
  ISBN-10: 0-9796726-3-5

  1. Faith and reason. 2. Belief and doubt.
3. Reasoning. 4. Decision making. 5. Conduct of life.
I. Title.

  BT50.T88 2008              211
                           QBI08-700036

Choose To Believe: A Practical Guide to Living Your Dreams
Copyright © 2008 by Alan Tutt
First Edition

All rights reserved.  No part of this book may be reproduced or transmitted, in whole or in part, by any means, electronic or mechanical, without the written permission of the publisher, except by a reviewer who may quote brief passages in a review.

Produced using OpenOffice Software from OpenOffice.org
Cover design by Archer-Ellison Design / BookCovers.com
Copy editing by Toni Edson & Lauree White
Printed in the United States of America

---

PowerKeys Publishing
1805 Walker Ave NW
Grand Rapids, MI 49504
www.PowerKeysPub.com
info@powerkeyspub.com

## Special Quantity Discounts

PowerKeys Publishing offers special quantity discounts, making our books ideal for sales premiums and incentives, corporate gifts, fund raising, and more.  Special customized versions are also available for specific needs.  Contact our Special Sales Department at the addresses above for details.

**Order 4 or more copies, get a 40% discount.**
**Order 20 or more copies, get a 50% discount.**
**Order 100 or more copies, get a 60% discount.**
**Order 500 or more copies, get a 70% discount.**

# What People are Saying About
# *"Choose To Believe"*

**This may be the best in terms of new, useful information I have heard in years. And I've read and heard plenty.**
— Robert Blake from Philly

You so clearly and simply explained Quantum Physics, that I FINALLY GOT IT!!! I was very, very, tired and exhausted yesterday when I came to work. I could barely wait until lunchtime to take a quick power nap. Instead of napping, I began to read your manuscript. I read your quantum explanation once, and it had such an impact on my brain that I had to read it again. During the second read-through, I, that is, my brain either dozed off or went to a completely different consciousness for just a split second or two. In that split-second, like a mini-dream, the theory and logic of Quantum Physics was literally shown to me. (I wonder if this is the vision-type of revelation that Daniel, of the Bible, experienced.)

It was like the Star Trek special effects of going "warp speed." I can only explain it as a brief picture or scene that, not so much visually, but more the essence of the theory that was "warped" into my brain. I don't think I've ever had an experience like that before, but I can only say the particles in my brain must have liked what I was reading and opened up a secret section of brain never used before, so that my brain could absorb it.

WOW!!! Thank you so much. If the rest of your manuscript is like the first few pages, OHMYGOSH!!

**Thank you for awakening the dormant parts of my brain.**
— Katie Shephard

Alan,

With your book, *"Choose to Believe,"* you have provided an enormous amount of information. To the point that I found my Self taking notes so that I may appropriately use them for myself and also in guiding others.

From your own personal experiences, you are bringing forth and expressing what you kNow to BE true, which comes from the inner Wisdom that we all have, and in doing so this will have a positive and magnificent ripple effect that will BE for the benefit of many.

I congratulate you for all of the above and in what I "believe" is a great book that you have written, and especially with the processes you presented to enhance the lives of others.

*"Choose to Believe"* **is for the best and highest good of all.**

It is time and well deserved.

Ilumine 2 Ao,

— Al Diaz

http://www.TheMiracleOfLove.com

Beliefs are the blueprints of a person's life and the single most important aspect to understand if you wish to take control of your life. This is why Alan Tutt's new book, *"Choose to Believe,"* **will probably be the most important book you read this year**.

At 220+ pages, it isn't a quick read, however it is educational, inspiring, thought provoking and potentially life changing.

My favorite section is where Alan takes you by the hand to uncover your current beliefs and then helps you create new empowering beliefs. He then goes on to show you many ways how to enforce these new beliefs into your life.

I've read hundreds of personal development books but still learned a wealth of new information. This is a book I will be referring back to many times and I'd recommend it to anyone who is serious about taking control of their future.

— Iain Legg

http://www.RealMindPowerSecrets.com

Alan writes so clearly, so smoothly, that even the most "difficult" subjects (the role of quantum physics in forming your reality, for example) become utterly simple. He'll have you wondering why these things ever seemed hard before. But while good explanations are crucial, they're not enough, and Alan knows this. So he also teaches you practical, proven methods and techniques for choosing more useful beliefs, and then making them a permanent part of your life. **With this book, Alan delivers what other teachers only promise.**

      — Charles Burke

      BullsEye-Living.com

Of the hundreds of books I've read, this has got to be in the Top 3! I've read about miracles before, but never have I found any material that clearly explains how they happened.

*"Choose to Believe"* not only reveals the deepest secrets of how beliefs can produce miracles in real life, but also provides undeniable proof and case studies to confirm the reality of its power.

**Anyone who reads this book will experience a miraculous transformation!**

      — Michael Lee, Persuasion Expert

      http://www.20DayPersuasion.com

I haven't come across a gem like this for a long time. I would like to avoid using phrases like "pure gold," or "a treasure trove of information," but I can't because the book is exactly this. **If you really care to change your life for the better, this book is for you.**

Within its pages, you will find answers to not only questions we all have about our world, but also solutions to many problems and practical advice on how to perform miracles in your own life, including setting your financial thermostat. Get your copy soon.

      — Irena Whitfield

      http://www.TheCassiopeia.com

Dear Alan,
Your books and MP3's were outstanding and very helpful. The *"Choose To Believe"* book I have read 3 times; the whole 220+ pages of it. **This is the book that hit home with me and inspired me to turn my life around.**
Alan, I don't know how to say thank you enough for your help and wisdom that came through your books. It has changed my thinking around in all aspects of life, love, trust, and especially BELIEF, which I had so many problems with.
You see, I had a very challenging life from the moment I was born. I was born 3 months earlier than I should have, I experienced: abandonment; rejection; sexual, verbal, emotional and mental abuses since I was a tiny little girl; I witnessed slaughter of people in front of me during the war in my country, including the horror of a baby's head being blown out with a machine gun, splattering its brain all over its mother and me. My family and I escaped death with the count-down to 4 — by assassination for attempting to escape the country, but were stopped. Two days after that, my family and I did manage to escape from our war-torn country, in the middle of winter I might add, risking the possibility of freezing to death. We walked for 2 nights and 3 days getting lost, realizing that we walked around a huge mountain three times, however, we finally found our way to a neighboring country safely and without any major problems; I was only 9 years old at the time.
Some time later, I married a Greek man whose mother, friends and the neighborhood Greek community did not approve nor accept me as I wasn't a Greek myself, and after 3 beautiful children, I felt I had enough of their prejudices, I applied for a divorce. I won't go on anymore as my story would take several chapters to tell, and 100's of pages to read, however, the above experiences are just a short synopsis of my story. The fears, insecurities, self-doubts, distrust, anger, inability to believe and formulate meaningful relationships with some people was a burden that I carried with me all my life.

Your book, "*Choose To Believe*," forced me to question and analyze my thinking, values, attitudes and my inner core beliefs. It revealed to me how my interpretations of things were very self-defeating; I came to realize that it was I who attracted all those pains upon myself through my thinking and believing. How wrong was I? I now accept and believe that I am a spiritual being; a daughter of God, connected to the Universe and to all things of life with a more definite purpose in life for me. The affirmations helped me greatly.

I turned everything around and began to formulate new beliefs; new ideas and slowly letting go of old conditioned beliefs. I trained myself to rely on my instincts and prayers, and I seek for inner guidance to bring out the truth and reality about the issues before me, before I place any value and acceptance of it as the truth or belief.

The outcome of all this exercise is that now I am more at peace within myself; every day I tell my self that "My self-worth does not depend on other's acceptance or approval of me; I have to approve of me." Therefore, I now see things in a different perspective, I have a new level of thinking, my relationships with challenging people have wonderfully changed, I turned to God, and currently I'm reading the Bible (New Testament). I can now see that everything is "mind over matter" as to how one perceives the world, things, especially oneself; as James Alan said: "As A Man Thinketh, So Is He" (I think that's in the Bible as well).

**Alan, I have put all your theories and education into practice and tested them out — with the help of all the affirmations throughout your book. So far, all is working for me as I wished, prayed and hoped for, for so long.** I just needed some guidance and new perspective to put me on the right track. Every now and then, I slip back one step, but I also take 2 or 3 in replace of that one step.

I THANK YOU SO VERY MUCH WITH ALL MY HEART AND SOUL.

— Sincerely, Agnes (from Australia)

Alan's inspiring book is a 'mind-opener' as he delves deeply into ALL the aspects of our belief systems — which vary widely among individuals, cultures and backgrounds. He touches on the depth and breadth of our innate ideals and the functions of our beliefs, as well as offering proof to back up what he presents to you. This is not a casual read, so plan to spend some time, and **expect to be challenged, inspired, empowered and educated** by this book. Alan also bravely shared his painful past so that the reader could truly grasp the massive power of belief and experience the immense power of our thoughts much more vividly. It's not JUST a book of facts and information like so many we read these days, because Alan also shows you HOW to put everything to work in your own life, and that is priceless. I highly recommend this book for those seeking real guidance for life changes and improvements.

— Donna Maher, RN
http://DonnaMaher.com

**This unique book is unlike any other I've ever read before!** I found myself learning a lot and gaining inspiration from it! Now I realize that even though the intention-manifestation process works, one needs to BELIEVE in it to successfully use it. This principle explains the times when I got less than expected results because I was slightly doubting the intention-manifestation process. All spiritual powers operate by FAITH. This book has given me greater insight about reality creation and taken my understanding of consciousness to the next level!

— Enoch Tan, Enoch Mind Reality
http://www.MindReality.com

# Dedication

This book is dedicated to those who have sought *a reason to believe*, and do not want another line of fluff, or airy-fairy tales of magic genies and wishful thinking.

It is for these readers that I have spent my life researching, experimenting, separating fact from fiction, and organizing those facts into this book.

Enjoy!

# Acknowledgments

*"If I have seen further than others, it is because I stood on the shoulders of giants."* I'm not exactly sure where this quote originally came from, but it comes up in my thoughts often. Anything included in this book is here only because I have had brilliant people to follow.

At the top of this very long list is Dr. Joseph Murphy, who wrote numerous books about belief, including the one that opened my eyes to the possibility of miracles occurring within my own life, *"The Miracle of Mind Dynamics."*

I also owe a huge debt of gratitude to Max Freedom Long for his book, *"The Secret Science Behind Miracles."* It was his book that led me to search for the scientific basis behind what we commonly call miracles.

José Silva and his Silva Mind Control Method showed me an easy to use system that can alter what we believe and thus alter our life experiences. Following the basic principles he set forth, I was able to discover several other techniques not commonly used for this purpose.

Ernest Holmes and Charles Filmore both wrote many great books providing ample examples of faith in action. The religious organizations that sprang forth from their leadership (Religious Science and Unity, respectively) are both wonderful sources of inspiration and comfort.

Although lesser known, Phineas Parkhurst Quimby also discovered the immense Power residing within us all, and taught many others how to tap into this Power, including Mary Baker Eddy, who later founded the Christian Science movement.

Milton Erickson, known as the father of modern hypnosis, deserves special recognition for giving the world a means to help others alter their belief systems in ways that are subtle, yet powerful. John Grinder and Richard Bandler are also to be commended for codifying Erickson's techniques into the science of Neuro-Linguistic Programming (NLP).

Of course, those who provided information are not the only ones I wish to acknowledge. Those who provided inspiration and motivation were also vital to this book's production.

At the top of this list are my parents, Judy and John Tutt, for instilling within me the belief that I could accomplish anything I set out to do.

Leta Goff, of Kansas City, was also a tremendous inspiration during my life's darkest days. Acting as a "surrogate grandmother," she saw more potential within me than I did myself.

My wife, Linda Missad, demonstrated by example how to live by faith, and the miracles that can happen when you trust that all will be well despite appearances. Paying close attention to the relationship between her spoken thoughts and the events that followed led to many insightful revelations. That and her continuing faith in me have motivated me more than she could have ever foreseen. She has also been a tremendous help in preparing the manuscript for this book.

There are so many more who deserve recognition in one way or another. Al Diaz, Guy Finley, David Barron, Charles Burke, Andreas Ohrt, Jeff Staniforth, Iain Legg, Ray Dodd, Dan Poynter, Fred Gleeck, Jim Edwards, and a host of others who helped me over the past few years with the business side of writing and building a following online. It is only with their help that I have been able to attract several thousand loyal subscribers to my mailing list.

I also want to fully acknowledge Lauree White and Toni Edson, who helped me edit the manuscript, and Kimberly Leonard and Allen D'Angelo of BookCovers.com who have created a beautiful cover design.

# About the Author

Alan Tutt started out in life as an 'A' student, but soon fell into failure due to an overabundance of limiting beliefs. After years of struggle and hardship, Alan came upon a message of faith, and pursued a line of scientific research until it paid off in a long series of personal successes.

Now with over 25 years of experience, Alan spends his time presenting workshops and coaching individuals and businesses to help them find the underlying beliefs responsible for hardships and limitations, and helping them change those beliefs to manifest greater success and empowerment.

Alan continues to refine his techniques and maintains a blog at www.PowerKeysPub.com, where you will find many inspirational articles that have already touched thousands of lives all over the world.

## Other Books by Alan Tutt

Harmonic Prayer
Awaken the Avatar Within
28 Days to Effortless Success
Prosperity From the Inside Out
Treasure Map to Online Riches
Keys To Power Persuasion

## Audio Programs

EmBRACES Belief Entrainment System
A variety of guided meditations

All of the above may be found on the PowerKeys Publishing website, at www.PowerKeysPub.com.

# Table of Contents

# What This Book Will Do For You

W ithin this book, you will find the answers to many of the world's biggest problems. Poverty, sickness, discord, loneliness, depression, frustration, and 'bad luck' can all become distant memories.

This isn't a book offering mystical mumbo-jumbo, nor should you think of it as a father patting you on the back and saying "Don't worry, it'll all be okay" without a definite plan for *making* it okay.

Yes, it CAN be "made all better," and you can see your life transformed as if by magic, but you won't have to "step out in faith" without a good, solid reason why.

Our society has recently seen a resurgence of an ancient concept called "The Law of Attraction," which basically says that your consciousness has the power to create change in the world around you without direct physical involvement. To many, this smacks of pseudo-science and fairy tales that fool the innocent and gullible.

> *"Any sufficiently advanced technology is indistinguishable from magic."*
> — *Arthur C. Clarke, "Profiles of The Future"*
> *English science fiction author (1917–2008)*

Nicola Tesla demonstrated many electrical devices that seemed magical at the time. The communication of sound across miles without wires was thought impossible before he demonstrated the principle of electromagnetic transmission. Modern radios, TV's, and cell phones are based on this one scientific principle. We use the same principle to communicate with satellites in outer space.

Imagine the surprise a primitive caveman might feel upon seeing something as simple as a tape recorder, or a cigarette lighter. These things just don't exist in his world. They aren't possible as far as he knows. You would be just as surprised to see some common item from the 24th century.

Just because we do not now understand the scientific principles behind something does not invalidate the phenomenon. In order to learn, we must be open to the possibility that we do not yet know everything, and that something we think we know may not be true at all.

> *"The great tragedy of Science — the slaying of a beautiful hypothesis by an ugly fact."*
> *— Thomas H. Huxley,*
> *English biologist (1825—1895)*

Many strange things exist in our world. Things that do not fit neatly into the accepted theories of science. If we are to call ourselves intelligent beings, it's imperative to accept the reality of what actually happens and not be swayed into thinking "it's only superstitious nonsense," as many scientists would try to convince you.

At one time, all intelligent people KNEW the world was flat and that the Sun revolved around the Earth. We now believe something different because new information has come to our awareness. Our current scientific understanding of how the universe works could also be proven wrong as more information comes into our awareness.

With so many people throughout history telling us that our beliefs affect the world around us, it's high time we take a good look at what might be supporting these claims and investigate the possibility of developing a technology to put these principles into action.

This book does exactly that.

Within these pages, you will find scientific evidence supporting the claims that our beliefs affect the world around us. This evidence comes from several fields, such as quantum physics, molecular biology, medical science, and scientific research into the phenomena of faith healing, ESP, and mind over matter.

Although this book has a lot of scientific information, I've taken the time to write in a relaxed style so that anyone who remembers their high-school education can understand it.

The concept of faith is central to most religions. Many books have already been written about what each religion teaches regarding the power of faith, and so this book spends very little time repeating what may be found in other resources.

You will find references to other resources, allowing you to extend your study if you feel the desire to do so. In fact, I have included a special resource section in the back of this book specifically for that purpose.

All this, however, is merely to provide a starting point. After all, what good is knowing about the power of belief if you can't do anything with it?

The majority of this book is devoted to helping you use the power of belief in your own life. You will find an easy way to discover what you believe on multiple levels, and how you can change those beliefs to support a more empowered life.

I have included many different techniques for you to use. Included here are not only the classic methods of belief change such as affirmations, visualization, hypnosis, and prayer, but also techniques from the relatively new fields of Neuro-Linguistic Programming (NLP) and conversational hypnosis. With these, you can literally change what you believe within minutes.

You will also find in this book useful guidelines to help you get the most from your efforts. These guidelines come from my own experience using the power of belief, as well as the experiences of many others. This way, you'll benefit from the many mistakes I and others have made and thereby have a more enjoyable time yourself.

In Chapter 7, you'll read about several people who have used the power of belief to make changes in their lives, so you can see how to bring this together into real-life situations. As you read about how they used the power of belief, I invite you to imagine using the same power in your own life.

Helping others is a natural desire we all have. That's why Chapter 8 is focused on showing you how to help other people change their beliefs. Even if you're happy with your life the way it is now, you may want to read this book to learn how you may help those around you improve their lives.

There are two pathways to helping other people with their beliefs — directly and indirectly. Helping them directly may be accomplished by sharing this book and the techniques it contains with them. This pathway is familiar to most of us.

Helping someone indirectly can be realized through the way you phrase things when you speak to them. We normally do this unconsciously and with unpredictable results. By learning some techniques from conversational hypnosis, you'll be able to take conscious control over the way you speak to others and by extension, the way you affect their beliefs.

Through all this, you will find out why so much 'common wisdom' is just plain wrong, what the real truth is, and how to put it to practical use. You'll find out why it seems that the harder you work, the less successful you become. And how you can reverse the process, become immensely successful in everything you do, and have oodles of fun doing it.

You'll find the real secret to miracles, and why there will never be "One True Religion." In addition, you'll find out why so many people believe the silly superstitious things they do, and why horseshoes and rabbits' feet work for some people, but not for others.

I'm excited about the possibilities awaiting us as we begin to work together through this book. How about you?

Let's go ahead and get started, okay?

# Chapter 1: Why Beliefs Matter

W e all have many different beliefs about many different things. We have beliefs about ourselves, about what we are capable of doing and what we *deserve*. We have beliefs about other people and whether we can trust them or not. We have beliefs about the world in general and what we can expect to happen in various situations. We have beliefs about specific situations, such as the Tuesday morning meeting with an important client, our next vacation, and the first time we fell in love. We also have beliefs about the ultimate nature of the universe and where we fit in.

All of these beliefs influence the way we live our lives and the decisions we make. There is also substantial evidence suggesting that our beliefs are so powerful, they shape the events that happen in the world around us.

Let's take a look at a few examples which demonstrate the true power of beliefs in our world. I think you may be surprised to discover the amount of influence beliefs have over everything you experience.

## *Practical Examples*

The most obvious example of the effect our beliefs have in our lives can be found in the decisions we make.

Let's say that two different companies would like to hire you. The first job is with a local company and offers a salary that is 50% more than you currently earn. The second job is with a company in another state and offers to double your current salary.

When making this kind of decision, we usually weigh the pros and cons of each choice, considering factors we *believe* are important.

For instance, do we really believe that the outfit we happen to be wearing when we get the news makes any difference in our decision?  Probably not.  But factors such as the company's location, the salary offered, and our chances for promotion are usually believed to be important, so we take those into consideration.

If we believe that important factors include the personalities of our potential co-workers, or the alignment of the stars on the proposed starting day, then we would consider such information before making a final decision.

If you're like most people, you believe you're worth more than you're currently being paid, yet may have trouble believing you're worth twice as much.  This incongruity may cause you to back away from such an offer, thinking that "it's too good to be true."

Also involved in this example are your beliefs about your ability to succeed and thrive in new experiences.  If you believe it's likely for you to fail when away from your friends and family, you'll be less likely to take the job in the other state, and will probably stick with the local company.  However, if you feel confident in your ability to rise to the challenge (i.e.- if you believe you could be successful after moving away), then that's another matter entirely.

Whether we feel good or bad about moving to a new state and leaving friends and family behind comes from our beliefs about those specific relationships and the beliefs we have regarding relationships in general.

If you have difficult people in your life, do you believe it would be good to leave them behind, or do you believe it's important to resolve those differences before moving on?  These "universal beliefs" affect almost every decision we make.

When considering the possibility of joining a new community, do you believe that the people there will accept you, or do you believe they may reject you instead?  Do you believe it's easy to make new friends, or do you believe that true friends are hard to find?  Most of us aren't consciously aware of these beliefs, yet we respond to the overall *feeling* they produce within us on a subconscious level.

Many of these same beliefs influence our decisions in other areas of life as well. Our beliefs about how easy it is to make new friends usually influence our decisions in romantic relationships too. If you believe it's easy to make new connections with other people, you'll approach your love relationships differently than someone who believes new connections take months to form.

Someone who believes intense relationships never last may back away from an intensely enjoyable relationship simply because they believe it will end quickly and don't want to be hurt in the process. Rather than responding to the situation as it is, they respond to what they believe will be true in the future.

Most of us have beliefs about what is 'normal' in any given situation. This tends to make us suspicious when something is "too good to be true." Even though we may be getting everything we ever dreamed of and more, we start looking for the problems we believe MUST be there, subconsciously sabotaging the situation because we don't believe it can be that good.

These beliefs about what is 'normal' will also motivate us to improve a situation we feel is lacking. This is one reason why those who focus on a lack of success in their lives will often be motivated to work harder to produce a better result. As long as they believe that success is possible, they tend to experience the success they believe is 'normal'. This is one example of how a person can get a positive result from negative thinking.

Already, we have practical evidence of how our beliefs affect all areas of our life through the influence they have over our decisions. If we've been happy with the decisions we've made over the course of our life, then we can be satisfied with the beliefs supporting them. But if our decisions have left a trail of casualties in our wake, with bridges burned and opportunities lost, then choosing a new set of beliefs seems to be a worthwhile endeavor.

Let's see what else we can find.

## Support From Science

In today's global society, we've almost made a religion of science. We're tired of the BS claims from all the 'snake oil' salesmen coming to our door and promising fame and riches if we only trust them and use their product. Before we accept any new theory nowadays, we check to see what science has to say about it.

And those with a *critical eye* even look upon science itself with suspicion. After all, how far can you trust a group of people who claim to know how the universe began 14 billion years ago after only 200 years of quality observation from a single viewpoint (Earth)? That's like watching an arrow fly for 2 seconds then claiming to know where it was 4 years ago! It may have been moving in a straight line the whole 2 seconds, but you really don't know what happened yesterday.

Not so long ago, all respectable scientists KNEW the Earth was flat and the sun revolved around it. Today, we consider such theories nonsense, and forgive the old scientists because they lacked sufficient information. However, we must always remember that there may still be huge volumes of information modern science does not yet know.

Despite this, science generally produces reliable results. On a fundamental level, the scientific process is one of observation, logic, hypothesis, and experimentation. If you start with verifiable evidence and proceed with logic, you can create a hypothesis (an educated guess) about what caused the things you observed.

With a working hypothesis, you can construct an experiment to verify whether your hypothesis is correct or not. However, if there is something fundamentally wrong with your experiment, such as important variables not being considered, the results you get may suggest an inaccurate conclusion.

Only when all involved variables are taken into consideration will scientific experimentation produce a reliable conclusion. However, every failed experiment is an opportunity to learn more about the phenomenon being studied. As you will later discover, until science considers the variable of belief, any experiment performed MUST become suspect and any conclusions reached from such an experiment may be inaccurate.

The principle of leverage came from this scientific process. We all learned in school that with a lever, you can lift a ten pound object using only one pound of force, but in exchange, you have to move the lever ten times as far. Depending on the lever's size, you can get more or less amplification of force, but the principle is the same regardless of the type of lever. Furthermore, the principle works for everyone, and it works all the time. Otherwise, it would not be a scientific principle.

This leverage principle was used to build Stonehenge, the pyramids around the world, and to erect the stone statues on Easter Island. It continues to be used today in all modern construction. And all of this from one simple little principle!

## *Quantum Physics*

Science continues to study all aspects of the universe, from the very big (astrophysics) to the very small (quantum physics). At both extremes, science stretches beyond the limits of technology and its ability to measure things into the realm of theories and pure logic. This means they can't actually PROVE that what they say is true, but it certainly sounds good. Over time, some theories are proven to be valid while others are shown to be inaccurate.

Early scientists proposed the idea that if you were to divide something into smaller and smaller particles, you would eventually get something that could not be subdivided any further, which they called the "atom." Each type of material, such as iron, calcium, or oxygen, had it's own unique atom, which was supposedly stable and unchangeable.

Over time, that belief changed, and scientists eventually found a way to subdivide the atom into electrons, protons, and neutrons. Today, scientists are discussing so many new subatomic particles, it's like there's another whole universe in there!

Without getting into too much detail, we need to be aware of the unpredictable, almost mystical, nature of these new quantum particles. It seems scientists have proven that these particles can do things once believed impossible, such as being in two places at the same time, going backwards in time, and displaying a kind of 'synchronicity', suggesting that two particles are connected even when separated by vast distances. For more information on the experiments which led to these findings, I recommend you read Michael Talbot's "*The Holographic Universe*."

Quantum physics research has given rise to the concept that subatomic particles are not really particles at all. A true particle would be something solid, fixed, and always the same. Sometimes these subatomic things *appear* to be particles, and other times they *appear* to be some sort of wave, like sound, or a wave on an ocean. One way to visualize this dual nature would be to think of a single stone moving in many directions at once. Because of this, things on the subatomic level are called "quanta" (plural for "quantum") instead of particles.

What is astounding scientists is that these quanta only appear to be particles when they are being observed. Otherwise, they seem to be a type of wave. This has happened so often, it even has a name — the "Observer Effect." The only sensible explanation is to say that on a fundamental level, matter responds to consciousness!

Science loves mathematical formulae, since they help to predict what will happen in various situations. In the case of quantum physics, those formulae may be familiar to a professional gambler because they are based on *probabilities*. Scientists have no way to predict exactly where a quantum particle will be at any given time, and according to the Heisenberg Uncertainty Principle, it's *impossible*.

What this means to us is that the old belief about the universe being a stable, predictable system is no longer a valid assumption. If everything you see is made up of these tiny particles, and the particles themselves can go anywhere at any time, then what's to stop your chair from jumping to the ceiling, or a fancy new watch showing up on your wrist?

Are these quantum irregularities responsible for the various miracles and paranormal events that have been reported throughout history? And what directs the course of these subatomic particles, their unpredictable motions, and consequently the world we see around us?

The current theory believed by most scientists is that all the unpredictable events on the quantum (subatomic) level balance each other out to form the (more or less) predictable universe we see around us. Only time and experimentation will prove whether this theory is true or not.

In the meantime, many scientists are proposing theories that echo those of ancient mysticism. Concepts such as "we are all connected on a fundamental level" and "the universe responds to thought" have been around for thousands of years, and now science is starting to give serious consideration to the validity of these ideas. Maybe the ancient mystics and spiritual seekers, who were more intuitively inclined, simply knew things that science is only now beginning to confirm.

One such scientific theory centers around something called "The Zero-Point Field," which is described as a vast energy field filling the entire universe. According to the scientists, if you used Einstein's Mass=Energy formula ($E=MC^2$) to convert all the matter in the entire known universe into energy (much more than 1000 atomic bombs), the Zero-Point Field would match that in every single cubic inch of space. Many ancient mystical texts refer to the universe as "a vibrating sea of energy."

Now, try to imagine that much energy in every inch of your body! The scientists say that the only reason we don't notice this is because it's always there and we have nothing less powerful to compare it to. This is easy to understand when you think about trying to determine how high up an object is, like a shelf on the wall. Unless you know how high up the floor is, you cannot know how high the shelf *really* is.

One of the most respected scientists in the field of quantum physics, David Bohm, describes the universe as a continuum, with everything connected like your hand is connected to your arm. One example he uses is a whirlpool in a river. It may appear to be a separate thing, but it's still the same water, just moving in a different way.

Bohm also claims that consciousness and matter are simply two forms of the same thing. He says there is no fundamental difference between your mind and the world around you because they are interconnected and form a unified whole. Virtually every mystical and religious text to date has said in one way or another that "we are all one with God."

Despite our many technological advances, we still do not have any equipment capable of taking an atom's picture. When scientists talk about measuring something "down to a single atom," they are depending on the validity of mathematical assumptions rather than direct perception. Until we can see atoms directly and verify exactly what is being measured by scientific equipment, we cannot KNOW whether those assumptions are accurate or not. For now, scientists are merely "acting on faith" in these areas.

Quantum physicists themselves agree that their theories are only conceptual models of reality, and not a true description of reality itself. What makes the theories useful is the fact that they have been able to explain certain phenomena, and have helped in the production of extremely small computer circuits and other technological advances.

The implications suggested by quantum research are truly staggering! Maybe there is something to the old mystical teachings, and maybe our minds really do have an influence on the world around us. If it is actually possible for us to direct the course of our lives using our minds alone, then the only question left is *"How?"*

## *Molecular Biology*

What happens inside an atom will never be as fascinating as what happens within our own bodies. The field of molecular biology (the biology *inside* a living cell) bridges the gap between the two sciences.

Molecular biologists study the way living cells sustain life. To do that, they study proteins and other molecules, which are organized collections of atoms. The relatively new science of quantum physics has opened up a whole new way of thinking about the life inside a cell, which in turn has opened up a new way of thinking about life itself.

One of the leading scientists in the field of molecular biology is Bruce Lipton, author of *"The Biology of Belief."* In his book, Dr. Lipton provides a very clear and easy to understand description of what happens within living cells and how it translates to life as we know it.

Quantum physics tells us that the atoms within our cells are tiny, interconnected energy systems which form a continuous whole rather than discrete particles interacting with each other. When molecular biologists consider this, they realize how the processes responsible for producing life are not a series of individual activities that can be manipulated separately with drugs, but are a beautifully choreographed symphony, where everything responds to everything else.

As an example, when the body is dealing with an infection, it releases specific chemicals within a limited area to trigger a healing response. A single chemical may have different functions in different areas of the body, yet it is only released where it is needed. The same is true with many other bodily chemicals.

When prescription drugs are taken, they are dispersed throughout the body. Although these drugs usually produce the desired result, they also produce side effects because of the indiscriminate release in unrelated areas. In most cases, the side effects are minimal, but not always.

In 2000, the "*Journal of the American Medical Association*" published the results of a study conservatively estimating that prescription drugs accounted for more than 120,000 deaths in the United States annually and was the third leading cause of death. In 2003, another study found prescription drugs to be responsible for more deaths in the USA than anything else, including cancer and AIDS, causing more than 300,000 deaths per year.

With statistics like these, you have to wonder how the medical profession is able to help as many people as they do.

Dr. Lipton further explains why our DNA does not control our lives the way many scientists would have you believe. Research experiments have proven that DNA is only a collection of potentials, and the environment in which we grow and live determines which of those potentials are actually realized and which potentials are not.

The Human Genome Project discovered that we have far too few genes to account for the many complexities within us. In fact, we have about the same number of genes as the average rodent, and not many more than a microscopic worm. Reports of such things as a "math gene," or a "psychotic gene," or an "ADHD gene" must be false, unless the microscopic worm has them too.

This realization led to the conclusion that there are many different factors which determine exactly how our bodies grow and behave. Heredity is only one factor among many helping to shape our bodies during our lifetimes, and even how long those lifetimes will be.

At least one author has taken these concepts and surmised that it may be possible to stop the aging process altogether and extend life indefinitely. Anet Paulina, in her book "*Transcend the Aging Process*," combines the concepts taught by Dr. Lipton and others with theories from quantum physics in a very intriguing presentation.

This has profound implications, especially if some quantum physicists are right in saying that our thoughts are intimately connected to the rest of the universe.

## *The Placebo Effect*

While all this information about the foundations of life and the universe is nice to know, the question we are intensely interested in answering is how these microscopic events translate to real world experiences?  Does the unpredictable nature of things on the quantum level lead to any unpredictability on the conscious level in which we live?  And more specifically, can we choose to activate specific changes?

In medical research, it is common to test the effectiveness of a new treatment by comparing it to an inert, functionally worthless placebo.  A placebo may be a sugar pill, a bread capsule, an injection of sterile water, a physical manipulation, or anything that resembles the new treatment being tested.  Even surgery has been used as a placebo, where surgeons simply open up the area being 'treated' and sew the patient back up again without doing anything else.

In any given research study, the people participating as test patients (the subjects) are given either the real treatment or a placebo by the medical staff.  The subjects are never told whether they are receiving the real treatment or the placebo.  In a 'double blind' study, the medical staff themselves do not know which they are administering to the patients.  In ALL cases, the researchers who set up the studies *always* know which is which, and tally the results afterwards.  Even if no-one else has a belief about the drug being tested, these researchers cannot be eliminated from the experiment, and their beliefs must be taken into consideration.

In some cases, a research study is set up to find out how often the condition being treated goes into a natural spontaneous remission, by including a test group that receives absolutely no treatment whatever.  This also provides us with information on how effective the placebo itself is in treating the condition.

Over the years, it has been found that placebos are very effective in treating many types of conditions, especially pain.  Other conditions where placebos have been proven to be effective include allergies, arthritis, asthma, cancer, the common cold, depression, diabetes, motion sickness, multiple sclerosis, Parkinsonism, ulcers, and warts. An average of 35% of all patients receiving placebos have reported feeling as much relief from their conditions as patients receiving traditional treatment. This healing response to placebos is called "the placebo effect."

The effectiveness of any placebo depends upon the beliefs of both the medical personnel giving the placebo and the patient receiving it. If the doctor giving the placebo believes it will be effective, the patient is more likely to believe in it as well. When the patient believes the placebo will produce dramatic changes, it does, and when the patient is uncertain about the promised cure, the results are equally dismal.

In general, the form in which a placebo is given has a great deal to do with it's effectiveness. Injections are generally perceived to be more effective than capsules, which in turn are perceived to be more effective than pills. Surgery is perceived to be the most effective form of treatment, and produces the strongest placebo effect.

There have been many cases reported where a doctor prescribed what he or she thought was a miracle drug to a patient in need, only to find out *after* the patient was healed that the new drug was deemed ineffective for treating the condition for which it was administered.

One such case, as published in the "*Journal of Prospective Techniques*" in 1957, makes it very clear how quick and dramatic the placebo effect can be.

The patient, Wright, had an advanced cancer of the lymph nodes. Tumors the size of oranges filled his neck, armpits, chest, abdomen, and groin. Two quarts of milky fluid were being drained out of his chest daily. All the standard treatments had been used, yet Wright was not expected to live much longer.

Obviously, Wright didn't want to die, and when he heard about a new experimental drug called Krebiozen, he begged his doctor to try it. Even though the drug was being limited to patients with at least 3 months to live, Dr. Klopfer eventually relented and gave Wright an injection of the experimental drug. This was on a Friday, and Klopfer honestly did not expect Wright to live out the weekend.

By the following Monday, Wright was out of bed and on his feet. Upon examination, Dr. Klopfer found the tumors to be half their original size. Ten days later, Wright left the hospital apparently free of the cancer.

Several months later, research reports were being published that revealed Krebiozen had absolutely no effect on cancer of the lymph nodes. When Wright read the reports, he immediately had a relapse and was readmitted to the hospital.

At this point, Dr. Klopfer decided to try an experiment. He explained to Wright that the reports were in error and some of the earlier supplies of the experimental drug had lost their potency in transit. He went on to say that he had a newer batch which was highly concentrated and so strong they had to take precautions before administering it. In actual fact, Klopfer was bluffing and intended to inject Wright with sterile water — a placebo.

Despite the bluff, the healing response was real. Once again the tumors in Wright's body vanished in record time.

Wright remained cancer-free for another two months, until the American Medical Association announced that Krebiozen was completely ineffective in the treatment of cancer. At that point, Wright's tumors came back with renewed vigor and he died two days later.

Suggestion has a powerful influence on the effect of any treatment. Several studies have found that a person receiving a stimulant introduced as a sedative would become drowsy and fall asleep. Just as surely, a person receiving a sedative introduced as a stimulant would perk up as if the drug were a real stimulant. This clearly shows that our belief in a drug has a greater effect than the drug itself.

## *Faith Healing*

Since we have found that the effectiveness of placebos depends on the faith a patient has in them, and a patient's faith in a drug has more of an impact than the drug itself, then what does science have to say about faith healing in general?

When scientists set up a new research study, they attempt to eliminate all variables from the process except the ones for which they are testing. This is intended to produce a clear picture of the impact those variables have on the treatment being tested.

For instance, when science tests the effect placebos have on healing, they eliminate all variables they cannot control, such as the personalities or reputations of different healers, and the environment in which healing takes place. They do this by making sure these variables are the same in all cases.

As a result, science only tests healing performed in a hospital-type setting, using medical personnel with no outstanding reputations and very little charisma. Dull, bland, and boring. Nothing to get excited about.

There's nothing wrong with this, but it does limit the information science can collect. Some studies have shown dramatic evidence for the effect of faith on healing, and yet other studies have shown no correlation between the two. The only conclusion science can make with the current information is that there's a good chance faith healing is real, and there are other variables involved which have not yet been accounted for.

Medical science has come under attack for not adequately studying the effects of faith healing, with many claims of self-interest and too much attention to the financial bottom-line. This may be true, but the honest truth is that science doesn't have the resources to study everything, and faith healing just hasn't risen to the top of the list.

In the same way as some people believe that taking time to warm up before exercise is a waste of time, science in general doesn't consider faith healing to be an important subject to study.

Luckily for us, this isn't true of all scientists. There have been a few brave scientists who have spent significant time sifting through the charlatans and false healers, collecting information on authentic faith healers that can be used for future research.

Scientists like Jeanne Achterberg, author of *"Imagery in Healing,"* who has devoted herself to the study of shamanic healers in more primitive cultures. And scientists like Alfred Stelter, author of *"Psi-Healing,"* who has collected substantial evidence on genuine faith healers across the globe. Other scientists who have studied faith healing and miracle workers include Max Freedom Long, author of *"The Secret Science Behind Miracles,"* and Erlendur Haraldsson, Ph.D., author of *"Modern Miracles."* All of these provide solid, scientific proof that faith healing and 'mind over matter' are real.

Some of the most dramatic evidence for the power of belief can be found in cases of 'instant healing', where diseased or damaged tissues are transformed into healthy tissues within seconds. One such case was reported in Max Freedom Long's book, *"The Secret Science Behind Miracles."*

In this case, a man attending a small beach party fell and broke his left leg just above the ankle. In the group was a man who had seen similar breaks before and recognized the seriousness of the injury. Also in the group was a healer who gracefully took over the situation.

She gently pressed her hands on the place where the break occurred and chanted softly for a few moments, after which she became quiet. Minutes later she got up and announced that the healing was complete.

To the amazement of everyone there, the injured man rose to his feet and was able to walk normally. There was no indication that the leg had ever been broken.

Many of us have seen programs on television exposing certain psychic surgeons as frauds, but until I read Alfred Stelter's *"Psi-Healing"* I didn't realize just how prejudiced the scientific community can be in this area.

As an example, during an investigation of Antonio Agpaoa, a psychic surgeon in the Philippines, a Dr. Seymour Wanderman was given an offer to place his hands inside the opening of a patient's body to verify its reality, and later was offered the removed tissues for analysis. Both offers were refused, yet Dr. Wanderman later announced that the surgery was a hoax.

Unfortunately, this is not a rare case, and many scientists refuse to acknowledge the reality of evidence right in front of them, preferring to believe in a universe of perfect order and simple rules. Because we trust the intelligence of such scientists, many of us have been misled to believe these things can't possibly happen.

And yet, as we've already seen, the discoveries of quantum physics, molecular biology, and medical research have already proven that the universe is not quite so simple, and many things *do* happen that defy the old, and now outdated, laws of science. What we need to do is acknowledge the reality of such phenomena and find out what causes them.

## *Mind Over Matter*

Closely related to faith healing is the phenomenon known as psychokinesis (PK), telekinesis, or more commonly, 'mind over matter'. This is where a person is able to move physical objects using mental powers alone.

Some of the most famous experiments in this area were conducted by a scientist named J.B. Rhine at Duke University. Besides psychokinesis, Rhine also studied many other areas of what is generally called the paranormal, including ESP, telepathy, clairvoyance, and precognition. His work conclusively proved that everyone has some degree of psychic ability, although various factors alter the degree of success in any given situation.

In the many experiments conducted by Rhine, a positive result was recorded as a 'hit', and a negative result was recorded as a 'miss'. Tallied together, the percentage of hits to misses became each subject's 'score'. After many thousands of trials, the data was analyzed for statistical significance and the real truth became clear.

Rhine found that his subject's motivation affected the scores they achieved, as did their interest level in the experiments. Thus, the more *connected* the subject was with the experiment, the better they performed.

Whether a subject believed in the reality of psychic abilities or not was the most telling factor. Rhine called this the "sheep-goat" effect. Those who believed psychic abilities to be a natural occurrence performed much better than those who thought the subject was a waste of time.

Some of the strongest criticisms of Rhine's work revolve around the concept of chance. After all, even a broken clock is right twice a day. Statistically, a random series of guesses would be correct a certain percentage of times. For example, in experiments where a subject tries to sense which one of five cards his or her partner is holding, a random guess would be right about 20% of the time.

Over the course of Rhine's research, the average scores achieved by his subjects were only a small degree better than chance. Despite the fact that the results were statistically significant (in other words, they couldn't have happened by chance), critics tend to suggest that the small results *prove* psychic abilities are weak or cannot be trusted. However, this may be easily explained when you realize that Rhine himself believed the results would not show anything dramatic.

The main thing to notice about these experiments is that they prove scientifically that our consciousness extends outside our bodies and can affect the world around us, according to the belief we have in the process. They also demonstrate that we are all connected on a level beyond the physical.

In situations where belief is stronger, the results of such activity are proportionally more sensational. Take, for instance, the case of Sri Sathya Sai Baba, an Indian mystic, famous for the unending flow of materializations he produces "out of thin air."

A scientific investigation of Sai Baba, as reported in *"Modern Miracles"* by Erlendur Haraldsson, Ph.D., reveals that practically everyone who has come into contact with Sai Baba has observed materializations of some kind. Most have a locket or ring given to them by the miracle-worker himself.

There are several factors that tend to prove the validity of the materializations produced by Sai Baba. One is the continuous flow of gifts given since the 1940's, many of which are composed of precious metals. Another is the fact that no one has yet detected any fraud in his presence. It stands to reason that of the many scientists who sought to disprove the claims of miracles, at least one of them would have found some evidence of fraud if it existed. Since no one has, we can confidently conclude that the miracles are real.

The third point is the fact that he performs his miracles openly for all to see, with no restriction of any kind regarding photography of the events. In all cases, the cameras have recorded exactly what observers saw, proving that no type of 'mass hypnosis' was involved.

A fourth factor tending to prove the reality of Sai Baba's materializations is his apparent ability to produce objects upon request, including fruits that are out of season and difficult to obtain in India. Of the foods Sai Baba is reported to produce, many are baked sweets that are very hot to the touch when given, as if they had just come out of an oven.

When asked how he produces these miracles, his answer is that he merely thinks of what he wants, imagines it, and then it appears. In this process, he does not need to imagine all the minor details, just the overall form of the object.

One example of this is when he pulled a statue of Krishna out of the sand for some visitors. While out for a drive along the seashore, the group stopped at a beach and began to discuss their visit to a local temple, where they had hoped to see a famous statue of Krishna. Sai Baba offered to show it to them, whereupon he drew a figure in the sand, reached in with both hands, and pulled out a magnificent golden statue. One of the visitors asked how it was done, to which Sai Baba replied, "I said to myself, let that image of Krishna, which is traditionally present in the minds of all these people, appear in the form of a golden statue."

Sai Baba performs many other types of miracles besides materializations. Reports of instant healing abound, as do reports of bilocation (appearing in two places at the same time), teleportation (the instantaneous movement from one location to another, usually separated by great distances), ESP, and telepathy. These reports have been followed up by responsible scientists and the claims hold up even under intense scrutiny.

There have been legends of others with similar abilities, not the least of which was Jesus Christ. With modern proof that such miracles do indeed happen, perhaps we have good reason to believe once more in the miracles of the Bible. If the miracles of Christ were accurately recorded, and not the product of exaggeration over time, then there's a good chance that his message was recorded accurately as well.

If this is true, then we may want to take a fresh look at the quotes where Christ tells us that "whatever you ask for in prayer, believe that you have received it, and it will be yours."

## *Religion*

Science hasn't always been considered the most reliable source of information. For thousands of years, religious leaders were regarded as the ones with the 'inside scoop' on the nature of the universe. Perhaps this is why science is only now starting to propose theories that support spiritual teachings which have been around longer than recorded history.

Some of the most widely available spiritual texts of ancient times are currently available in the Christian Bible. While there is much debate about how much the material has been edited over time, and whether translations have given us the 'true meaning' of the original languages, we can still see some very important messages in the text we have today.

One message clearly evident in today's New Testament is demonstrated by Christ repeatedly saying that "according to your faith is it done unto you." This quote appears in several cases of healing miracles, and is an ever-present theme in his teachings.

There are many other quotes mentioning the value of faith, especially as it relates to prayer. For instance, when the disciples were afraid of the stormy sea, Christ rebuked them for having weak faith and then commanded the wind and waves to be still, confident that the desired result would be forthcoming. And in several passages, Christ is quoted to have said (slightly paraphrased) "If you commanded this mountain (or tree) to cast itself into the sea, and did not doubt it would happen, it would be done for you."

Overall, the two most repeated messages attributed to the founder of today's Christian religion are about Faith and Love. This coincides very neatly with the discoveries of modern science as the core principles leading to a full and satisfying life. Other religions also teach that faith is a prerequisite to receive abundant blessings from God.

The development of religion is a vast and interesting topic. At its foundation, religion developed as a way for humanity to relate to the world around them. In some cases it sought to provide meaning and guidance for living, although in many cases it was a call for help from invisible sources.

Before organized religion, everyone had their own idea of how to gain this assistance. Some believed there was one great God responsible for everything. Others believed there were many gods and goddesses, as well as innumerable nature spirits who shared the responsibility of keeping the universe running smoothly. Some people believed that God required a great sacrifice before assistance would be granted, and others believed that God required the petitioner to meet some mysterious standard of purity. Still others believed that assistance could be obtained through the studious use of substances, such as oils, incense, and 'magic potions'.

When we step back and analyze the various processes used throughout history for gaining spiritual assistance, we find a single thread running through all of them — dependence on faith. Faith that a prayer will be answered, or faith in a process of working with spiritual forces.

## *Popular Literature*

In 1926, an intellectual by the name of Ernest Holmes wrote a textbook that formed a bridge between science and religion. That textbook was rewritten in 1938 and has been in continuous publication ever since. Countless other books refer to it and the philosophy it teaches. In fact, it became so popular, a movement called Religious Science formed around it. This textbook is *"The Science of Mind."*

If a book's value can be measured by the number of lives it changes for the better, then *"The Science of Mind"* can legitimately be called one of the most valuable books of the 20th century. Within it, Holmes presents a semi-scientific description of faith and the means by which it works. He also presents a very simple technique for altering faith in order to change circumstances for the better.

The core technique used by practitioners of *"The Science of Mind"* is one called "treatment." This is a process of altering your belief about a situation by affirming what you would like to experience, as if it were your current reality. Many people describe this as using "affirmations," or "affirmative prayer."

In 1948, a newspaper reporter named Claude Bristol wrote a much smaller book about the power of belief called *"The Magic of Believing,"* which has also been in continuous publication since its release.

As a newspaper reporter, Bristol never took anything at face value and sought to find proof of any claim before giving it any credence whatsoever. During his career, Bristol investigated many religious and spiritual events, as well as people in all walks of life.

He noticed that two people could do exactly the same thing and get two completely different results. After seeing this many times, he eventually concluded that it was a difference in belief which produced the different results. One person believed in success and the other believed in failure.

Bristol offers several techniques for changing beliefs in order to change outcomes. One of these techniques involves writing down your desired outcome on an index card and then every morning and evening visualizing yourself experiencing that outcome. Through continued exposure to the idea, your mind naturally adapts and begins to imagine your desired outcome as the most likely event to occur. Once you believe it, you'll see it manifest in your life.

Visualization has been written about in much of the popular literature of the last 50 years. A famous book, which focused almost exclusively on this topic, was "*Creative Visualization*" by Shakti Gawain. Visualization works on the same basic principle of conditioning your mind to believe your desired reality is likely to manifest.

In the last several decades, there has been a resurgence of new material based on very old ideas. Most of the material focuses on using unseen forces to create or alter circumstances, and reminds us of the old myths and legends about magic and wizards. And yet with the new discoveries of quantum physics and the fundamental nature of our physical universe, the idea of magic seems plausible again.

Recently, many authors have been writing about something called the "Law of Attraction." In essence, the "Law of Attraction" is a way of presenting the same concepts we've discussed in this chapter, and will continue to discuss throughout this book.

The "Law of Attraction" states that people experience physical and mental manifestations which correspond to their predominant thoughts, feelings, and beliefs, and that people therefore have direct control over reality and their lives through thought alone. Some authors claim that the concepts have been kept secret from the masses, yet as we've seen here, that hasn't been the case.

## *Conclusions*

Everywhere we look, we find evidence supporting the idea that our beliefs affect the world around us, and that they may even change physical reality itself. Whether science can verify this to be the case or not remains to be seen, but it certainly presents an interesting hypothesis to test.

While some of the possibilities presented in this chapter may appear extreme, it is clear that we can radically change our lives by choosing what to believe. Even if the only effect of changing a few beliefs is that we begin to make different choices, this alone will enhance our lives in countless ways.

But what if it really is possible to produce changes in the world around us merely by thinking about them and believing that the changes will happen? And what if the process of choosing a new set of beliefs can be quick and easy?

> *Jesus turned and saw her. "Take heart, daughter," he said, "**your faith has healed you.**"*
> *— Matthew 9:22*

> ***According to your faith will it be done to you.***
> *— Matthew 9:29*

> *I tell you the truth, if you have faith as small as a mustard seed, you can say to this mountain, "Move from here to there" and it will move.*
> ***Nothing will be impossible for you.***
> *— Matthew 17:20,21*

> *I tell you the truth, if you have faith and do not doubt, not only can you do what was done to the fig tree, but also you can say to this mountain, "Go, throw yourself into the sea," and it will be done.* ***If you believe, you will receive whatever you ask for in prayer.***
> *— Matthew 21:21,22*

> ***Everything is possible for him who believes.***
> *— Mark 9:23*

# Chapter 2: Examples of Belief in Action

You and I are about to get very intimate. In Chapter 1, we reviewed evidence suggesting our beliefs affect the world around us. Now we'll explore how that concept may manifest in your life.

No matter how much theory you read, the concepts we're talking about here just don't hit home until you see the connection for yourself. As the author, I debated with myself about how to do this effectively. It's not like a coaching situation, where you tell me about your life and I ask questions about what your beliefs were in each situation, helping you to realize the subconscious connections.

I considered telling a series of stories where the power of belief is commonly thought to exist. I thought about sharing case histories of my clients who have had amazing experiences demonstrating the awesome power of belief. I thought about covering the history of various belief systems.

Finally, I realized that none of these would convey the depth of understanding you need to get the most out of this book. If I'm going to make my message clear, I have to do whatever it takes. And to do that, I have to open my soul to you and show you how my own beliefs have directed the course of my life.

This also means I have to reveal parts of myself that are less than perfect. While I'd like to say I've perfected my life, let's face it — I'm human and have my own weaknesses. Like everyone else, I'm trying to be the best I can be, and there's *always* room to grow and develop.

Hopefully, you'll see elements in my story that have similarities to elements in your own life. If so, you may find yourself realizing on a more conscious level the way your beliefs affect your world.

## *Growing Up*

The beginning of my life was spectacularly uneventful. No bright star shining over my head. No fanfare. No crowds of people marveling at the inherent wisdom of a child.

Like most people, I don't remember the first few years of my life. My earliest memory is of my baby brother coming home from the hospital when I was four and a half. I remember holding him and playing with him.

During those early years, I absorbed much more than just motor skills and the basics of language. I absorbed a lot of what my parents said to each other and to me. I remember from later years how they would talk about money as though there usually wasn't enough of it, and we'd have to choose what to have and what to do without. I remember some of the fights they had with each other, and the way they worked together as a team. I remember the value they placed on family and keeping in touch with relatives, even if only once a year. I remember many comments about how smart I was.

Whatever happened in those early years, it shaped the core of my self-image, the concept I had of myself, and how I saw the world around me. From those experiences, I collected a set of beliefs about what was 'normal' and what I could reasonably expect to experience in life.

As I went through school, my teachers reinforced the belief my parents gave me about my intelligence. Their confidence in my intelligence directed me to get mostly A's. I could have earned even better grades (possibly straight A's), but I didn't feel it was worth the extra effort. My inner beliefs about what I could reasonably expect from life didn't support the concept of being overly successful, so why bother trying?

This shows us how two different beliefs can pull us in two different directions. I believed I was smart, and my grades tended to reflect this belief, but I also believed I would have a mediocre life where money was tight.

There is a common belief that smart people who get good grades in school will automatically earn lots of money in life. Since I've seen others who have experienced this, I see where the possibility does exist, however my life is proof that it's not always true. I struggled with money issues for much of my life, but I'm getting ahead of myself here.

Several times over the years, my parents commented on how my brother and I seemed to be "as different as night and day." Many times they told the story about how I was born with blond hair and blue eyes while Jarrett was born with dark hair and almost black eyes. Perhaps the difference in appearance led to a difference in treatment, which in turn led to our different personalities. Maybe it was something else. For whatever reason, we were taught to believe we were fundamentally different from each other.

Our belief that we were different may have been the main reason Jarrett didn't do as well in school, and has gone a completely different direction in his life. After all, if we were supposed to be different, and I did well in school, then Jarrett *had* to do poorly to "be who he was meant to be."

The same belief may have caused me to feel as if I didn't fit in with everyone else. Jarrett seemed to make friends more easily than I did, and since we were "as different as night and day" then it was 'logical' to assume that I wouldn't be as lucky. Whether it was logic or something else, that became my experience for many years. I felt like an outcast everywhere I went until I consciously chose to change the belief behind the feeling.

Personally, I see the connection between the beliefs we were taught at home and where we've both gone in life. He has simply focused on one subset of beliefs and I've focused on a different subset. Although our choices were originally subconscious, we now have the option to choose our beliefs consciously.

## *College Life*

Because I had done so well in school, everyone assumed I would go to college and get a degree, which supposedly guaranteed a good job and lots of money. This was in the 80's when the computer industry was booming, and I did have a keen interest in the design of computer circuits. Pursuing a career in electrical engineering seemed a natural choice.

My high school guidance counselor brought to my attention a scholarship program offered by DeVry Institute of Technology. According to my father, it would cost about the same to move away from home and attend DeVry (with the scholarship) as it would cost to stay at home and attend the local college. I was decidedly in favor of moving away.

The first few weeks were wonderful! The school didn't have dormitories, but it did have rental agreements with several apartment complexes. I was assigned to a two bedroom apartment with 3 other guys. My roommates seemed to be reasonably okay, and we had a blast exploring the Chicago suburbs.

It wasn't long, however, before the reality of the new situation sank in. When growing up, my parents never gave me much responsibility other than a few chores around the house. I assumed they didn't trust me to handle bigger tasks, and the resulting belief that I could fail made itself known during my time at DeVry.

To give you the complete story, I have to tell you that if anyone at that time had asked if I would fail, I would have scoffed at the idea. On the surface level, I believed I could handle everything thrown at me, yet on a deeper level, another belief waited for an opportunity to express itself.

The whole process started with two beliefs — there wasn't enough money, and money didn't come easily. These led me to conclude that I HAD to get a job (which in itself was a belief). That would have been okay, except I also believed (on a subconscious level) that I wouldn't be able to handle the responsibility.

Several people told me that the best job I could get was at a fast-food restaurant (Wendy's) for a little over minimum wage. I accepted their belief, and for the next ten years continued to see myself as someone who was worth a little over minimum wage.

Meanwhile, I also believed I was a good worker, and as a consequence, my boss at Wendy's continually scheduled me to work a full 40-hour workweek. My beliefs about being able to handle anything and my beliefs about not being able to handle responsibility collided (along with a belief that employers demanded greater loyalty than school) and produced a feeling that I couldn't refuse the extra hours.

Unfortunately, this pushed me beyond my limits, and I started oversleeping and missing classes. And not just the first class in the morning, but the whole day! I'm not sure what beliefs were involved, but for some reason, I felt too embarrassed about not getting to school on time and felt it was better to skip the whole day rather than be late. These days I look back on that and cringe.

Needless to say, my grades started to drop and the whole thing snowballed to the point where I felt like I didn't belong there any more. At the time, I believed I had failed so badly I couldn't pick up the pieces and turn it around. If I ever found myself in a similar situation again, I'd seek out someone who could see what I couldn't and get some qualified advice.

Back then, I believed that anyone who sought advice from another (such as a counselor) had failed as an individual. Today, I realize that we are generally blinded by our own beliefs and NEED to work with other people who can help us truly get to the heart of many matters we face.

## *Entering Adult Life*

By the time I left DeVry, I had a very strong belief in failure, which manifested in a wide variety of ways. Within a year, I lost my car, my home, and my girlfriend. I moved back in with my parents and tried to figure out what to do next.

I felt that my life needed a miracle. I started reading the Bible again and prayed, asking God to show me the truth behind Christ's miracles. In my prayers, I promised to share the truth with the rest of the world. Of course, those prayers came from a belief that God required a trade of this type. Today, I feel inspired to share what I've learned to help others avoid the hardships I went through, but that's another story.

I also pulled out some books that attracted my interest as a teenager and seemed to offer some of those miracles. Books on ESP, astrology, mysticism, and magick. I spent time in meditation and worked on developing my psychic skills. With practice, I gained an ability to sense objects around me. With more practice, I could feel when something was about to happen.

The books explained how psychic abilities were based on the presence of an invisible energy permeating the whole universe, much like the Zero-Point Field described by science today. The more I believed in the energy field around me, the more I noticed its presence.

Within a matter of months, I had the distinct impression that it was time for me to move on, although I didn't have a specific plan. My studies of intuition and ESP led me to believe that I could follow my impulses and trust them to lead me where I needed to go.

Not wanting to have a confrontation with my parents, I waited until a time when they were gone for the day before packing a bag and leaving. It wasn't until years later that I realized it happened to be Mother's Day. (Sorry, Mom.)

### Life as a Gypsy

As I look back on my life, I realize that one of the factors prompting me to make the decisions I did was a question in the back of my mind — "How do street people survive?" For me it wasn't an idle question, I really wanted to know because I thought I would have an important piece of the money puzzle if I knew how they did it.

Of course, I now understand I was asking myself the wrong question because I had an incorrect belief. If I really wanted to know how money was made, I needed to look towards people who had lots of it and ask how *they* did it. But my self-image (my beliefs about who I was and what I could become) didn't allow me to associate myself with rich people.

The end result was that I spent several months living on the streets. I went from Paducah, KY to St. Louis, MO to Indianapolis, IN to Kansas City, MO. I slept in homeless shelters and ate at food kitchens. I donated plasma for cash. I worked through a day-labor agency and hung out at the library and malls when I had nothing else to do.

Don't let this mislead you, though. It wasn't easy. There were many times I went without food for weeks at a time, and several times I asked for help (sometimes from churches) and was turned away because I was a young white male who supposedly already had all the advantages in life. If I had been a woman, or of a different race, people might have been more willing to help me out — reverse discrimination at work.

During much of this time period, which lasted the better part of a year, I approached every situation with a feeling of desperation. No matter how much I tried to 'think positive', and look for the silver lining around every cloud, it seemed the universe had conspired against me. I may have been thinking positively, but I believed negatively.

It always amazed me to hear so many others talk about everything as though it were the end of the world, yet they seemed to come out okay. What really upset me were the books I read about making money where the author said something like, "I didn't have ANY money to start, just $10,000 in the bank." Ha! I'd have been ecstatic if I had $10,000!

It didn't make any sense at all until I finally understood that it isn't our thoughts that create our world, it's our beliefs. Then I finally understood that those who 'spoke negatively' had beliefs about what was 'normal' that were far better than the beliefs I had about what was 'normal' for me.

Life changed for me one morning when I went into a mall to get warm after walking the streets all night. As I browsed through the bookstore, I discovered the writings of Joseph Murphy, who instantly became my favorite author!

As I stood there reading the words on the page, I felt an incredible sensation rise up within me. I learned to simply choose to believe that my prayer would be answered and to feel its reality within the moment. Instantly, I felt my whole body relax, and bursting forth was this unbelievable feeling of joy and satisfaction springing forth from the idea that I would be given enough money to rent a place and get myself back on my feet again.

That was about 10:30 in the morning. About 4:30 in the afternoon, I received the results of my 'prayer' when I found $70 on the sidewalk! With that, I was able to rent a cheap room for a week (*very* cheap, and *very* run down) and get a little food to keep me going. The very next day, I went back to the bookstore and bought three of Joseph Murphy's books, "*The Miracle of Mind Dynamics*" (the one I read in the store), "*The Power of Your Subconscious Mind*," and "*Your Infinite Power to be Rich*."

Today I own 14 of his books, with multiple copies of some of them. I like to buy multiple copies so I can give them away when I feel someone needs what the book offers.

## *Working With New Beliefs*

The core message in Joseph Murphy's books is the same message we're talking about now — that life reflects back to us the essence of our beliefs. When I first read this concept, I had been awake for nearly 24 hours and didn't have the mental energy to consider it beyond it's face value. I trusted it like you trust a chair to support you.

A few days later, after catching up on some much needed sleep and reading two of the books I had purchased, I tried using the same process again to see if it would bring more money. Results were not forthcoming a second time, so I assumed that either I hadn't done it correctly, or there was a flaw in the basic process.

What I didn't realize then was that I doubted the effectiveness of belief itself to produce any changes in the world around me. My intellect kept insisting that there MUST be an energy component to the process, since most of the books I studied had made the same assertion. It also didn't make sense that the physical world would respond to something so 'inconsequential' as thought. Those beliefs resulted in a series of hit and miss experiments as I continued searching for the 'true power' behind miracles.

Looking back on those experiences, I now realize that whenever my actions matched my beliefs about what was required for success, I saw successful results. And when my actions did not match my beliefs, I saw failure. When I believed that success required a concentration of mental energy, failure would result unless I strained myself mentally. When I believed that success required a 'light touch', then intense concentration would produce failure. I didn't fully understand the impact of subconscious beliefs, and so I continued to chase the wild goose.

I also realize now that some experiments failed even when my actions matched my beliefs exactly, simply because I believed failure was always a possibility. When you believe that "you don't always get what you expect," then the door is open for all kinds of things to happen.

## *Experiments in Belief*

Most of the time, I would experiment with simple things, like changing the weather. There was one summer in particular when I was living with someone who had a small garden and didn't want

to water it every day.  At one point, she commented that it would
be nice if it rained a little each day.  A few minutes of thoughtful
action did the trick.  Every day for the next three months, a small
amount of rain would fall from the skies.

Because I believed it to be so, it was more difficult to
increase my prosperity.  There were a few successes, however.
One such success occurred when I worked at a die-cutting shop, a
place that does finishing work for printers.  As a day-laborer hired
merely to do odd jobs, I had absolutely no control over the amount
of work that came into the shop, yet I was able to consistently
specify how many hours I would work each week.  At the end of
each week, my timesheet was consistently within a half-hour of
what I specified to myself at the beginning of that week.

I'll never forget the time I was talking to one of the press
operators about this and mentioned how I had decided I would get
48 hours that week (8 hours of overtime).  His reaction was, "We
don't even have enough work to keep us busy for 40 hours.
There's no way we'll get 8 hours of overtime!"  I smiled and
simply said, "We have no idea what other jobs are coming into the
shop.  We can only see what's here now.  There will be more jobs
coming in the next few days."

The other press operator (we had only two presses operating
on second shift) thought the idea was intriguing and was open to
the possibility.  Within a couple of days, a large job came into the
shop, which required foil stamping and needed to be out the same
week.  End result: the first press operator ended up getting only 40
hours that week and the second operator and I got 48 hours,
exactly what each of us *believed* we would get.

The next week, the second press operator and I were talking
about this and he suggested we go for maximum overtime.  I
thought it would be an interesting experiment and set my intention
accordingly.  By this time, my belief in the process was so strong,
I KNEW something special was going to happen.

Maximum overtime turned out to be 60 to 70 hour weeks for
months on end!  That special rush job was done so well we ended
up getting far more work from it than we bargained for!  My

paychecks were FAT to say the least! I was smiling regularly for the first time in years.

Notice here that I was not running a business. Nor was I a salesperson in this company. I was simply a day-laborer brought in to fill a low-level position. I also wasn't asking God to make things happen for me. I simply 'decided' what I wanted and felt assured (had faith) that I would get it. I didn't spend any time during the week thinking about whether I would get what I wanted or not, nor did I question the process. Once I set it in motion, I let it go and only checked at the end to verify it matched what I had specified.

From the many experiments I performed, I had solid proof there was a power I could use to consciously create changes in the world around me. Exactly how this worked was still a matter of debate, and I continued to test many different techniques and combinations of techniques for years afterwards.

A persistent belief in the involvement of energy factors led me to conclude that there were three keys to unlock the power of miracles. I knew that belief was one of those factors, but I also thought that mental focus was a factor, as well as something I called a "connection to Spirit." The formula was based on the notion that there is a form of spiritual Power constantly flowing through us, directed by our thoughts, feelings, and beliefs to create the events in our lives.

Having established this formula, I had a strong belief in the combination, creating many more successes than failures. It wasn't long before I started teaching others my system, which I called the *"Keys To Power."*

## *Relationship Success*

One of my successes was in manifesting the wonderful relationship I have with my wife, Linda. When I decided it was time to use my Keys To Power principles to manifest the 'perfect' relationship, I looked at the beliefs I had about relationships and asked myself what new beliefs would serve me better.

I would say that the most important new beliefs were: 1) as long as I use spiritual Power to create what I want, my life will always get better, and 2) every relationship is like a walk in the woods — sometimes you run into brier patches, but if you continue, you get to see glorious splendors. Both beliefs are based on faith — faith that there will be good times ahead.

Once I knew what pathway I wanted to take, I began working with self-hypnosis. I spent a few sessions a week programming the new beliefs into my mind so my reaction patterns would support the goal I set. Then, I started performing what I called creative daydreaming sessions.

In those sessions, I would enter a light to medium level meditative state. While in that state, I would affirm "I am now creating the future I want, and the images I play in my mind will manifest into my life. My inner mind knows the best way for this to happen, and it brings this about in the best way possible." For the next period of time (probably about 10-20 minutes) I would daydream about the relationship I wanted. I saw myself meeting someone who attracted me, and I saw her being attracted to me as well. I saw us spending lots of time together, and while seeing these things, I felt the emotions I knew I would feel when the events actually happened. I felt the most intense feeling of love I could imagine feeling. I felt the emotion of happiness, the emotion of desire, and all the other emotions that fill a good relationship. And yes, I daydreamed about wonderful sex.

After each session, I would feel very much at peace. Maybe there was a slight feeling of emptiness since the relationship was not there at the time, but I felt as if it would come soon enough. In essence, I felt as if I had spent some quality time with the woman of my dreams, and although she was gone, she would return later.

This feeling indicated that I was building a belief about what was 'normal' in my life. Since I felt that I had spent time in a loving relationship, it was easy for my mind to believe that such a relationship was normal. In turn, this belief helped direct events to create the relationship I wanted.

I continued to work with these sessions a couple of times a week for several weeks. Then I had to focus on other tasks, so I let it go. (This was during a period of rebuilding my life after some failed experiments.) In a few months, I met Linda, who is now my wife. As soon as I met her, I knew she was the one. Virtually everything I visualized, including many elements I had never experienced in a relationship, are now a part of our life together.

## *Prosperity Success*

Another success I'll share with you is my own personal prosperity. As you may remember, I grew up in a less than prosperous family. My parents often complained about how there wasn't enough money to do the things we wanted. They frequently reminded my brother and I that money didn't grow on trees, and that we could have only a limited number of the things we wanted. And when I got my first job, the school guidance counselor told me I was lucky to earn more than minimum wage, which was only $3.85 an hour at the time. I began to believe that I was worth only slightly more than minimum wage, and for the next 10 years or so, my experience reflected that belief.

I spent most of this time learning the principles behind the power of miracles. Needless to say, I spent a good portion of my efforts trying to increase my prosperity. Some of my experiments worked and I gained a few dollars, but others failed so miserably that I ended up losing everything.

As my belief in myself grew stronger, my experiments grew more and more successful. I began to believe I could be a good photographer and start a successful business, so I started pursuing freelance work in my free time.

A breakthrough came after I created my own 'not-so-subliminal' tape to help reprogram my inner beliefs about money and success in general. I simply recorded myself repeating dozens of affirmations about what I thought were important beliefs to have. When I played the tape in the background while doing other things, it became subliminal since I wasn't focused on listening to the affirmations.

An even bigger breakthrough came when I realized I could achieve much more, and used creative pretending to manifest greater prosperity. In those creative pretending sessions, I imagined owning a business which paid me a large, regular income and didn't require my personal involvement on a day-to-day basis. As I exercised, I pretended that my company was being handled by employees, and when the phone rang, I pretended it was a big order coming in.

At the time, I had no idea what kind of business it would be, but I knew it could happen simply because I was creating it. Each time I pretended I was a successful business owner, the idea felt more and more natural, and my belief in its possibility grew to the point where it felt not just possible, but quite likely!

In the following months, many people suggested I should start a website to teach others the principles I used. I had no idea how to create a website, and frankly, I didn't want to learn, so I resisted the idea. However, the more the idea was suggested to me, the more I believed it to be the manifestation of my creative pretending. Sometimes you just have to pay attention to what life is telling you.

What got me off my butt and online was an idea I heard while listening to the audio version of *"One Minute Millionaire"* by Robert G. Allen and Mark Victor Hansen. I heard that there were website services to help you create an instant Internet storefront using a point-and-click interface. The idea intrigued me, especially since the authors claimed it would generate a passive income with no day-to-day personal involvement. Although the resources they listed were no longer available, and the process wasn't as easy as they said, I did find a way to set up a website using a point-and-click interface. And thus, my first website (KeysToPower.com) was born. (It's changed a lot since then.)

One thing led to the next, and within a month, I was making money online. The more I learned, the more money I made. The nature of the Internet allows quick, cheap testing of advertising, impossible in any other form of business. And although I made many mistakes and spent a ton of money on my education (buying ebooks, software, and marketing courses), the business was "in the black" (had earned more than I had spent) in less than 6 months. Almost impossible with any off-line business!

The more I learn, the more my business continues to expand. Each time I write a new book, I create a website for it and list it on my central website (PowerKeysPub.com) where all of my products are sold. Following that, I announce the new book to my mailing list, and it goes from there. Pretty soon, I'll start publishing books by other authors, hiring employees to handle the day-to-day activities, and pursuing those activities I enjoy most.

None of this would have happened if it hadn't been for my creative pretending sessions helping me believe it was possible.

## *Personal Observations*

As we discuss various ways beliefs affect the events around us, you will notice that it really doesn't matter WHAT you believe, you'll find evidence in your experiences to support your beliefs. Those who believe in flying saucers will find evidence of their existence, and those who believe in the inherent goodness of people will experience kindness wherever they go.

Anyone who believes life is a series of lessons to be learned before moving forward will experience a series of difficulties (lessons), repeating until that person feels they have learned the lessons involved. Another person who believes life is meant to be fun won't experience as many difficulties, nor will the difficulties be repeated.

Psychologists tell us that this is only a matter of perception and the actual events themselves do not change. The only way to prove it one way or the other is to keep track of the frequency, type, and severity of difficulties experienced, as well as a record of the many beliefs held by the subjects at each point in time. I have not yet seen any formal, scientific study performed to collect this information, and therefore, we cannot yet take the psychologists' statements as anything more than opinion.

Until such a study is performed, we must be content to rely upon our personal observations and judge for ourselves the validity of these ideas. I urge you, dear reader, to join in the grand experiment and keep copious notes about your beliefs and your experiences, so we may validate the reality of this theory.

As you keep track of your beliefs and experiences, you may also notice that beliefs usually remain dormant until they are activated by an experience. That experience may be an action, a feeling, a situation, or just about anything else. It's like a T=>R (T leads to, or produces, R) equation, where T is the trigger and R is the response produced by your beliefs. For example, when you take an aspirin (T), the pain subsides (R). That's how placebos work.

## *The Placebo Effect Revisited*

We've already taken a good look at what's known as the "placebo effect" and how it triggers the healing response within your body. There are many people who feel the same thing occurs in alternative healing methods such as when wearing copper bracelets, or using magnets, crystals, or pyramids to 'charge' the body with healing energy.

All such 'energy therapies' tend to be assigned to this category since science hasn't been able to establish the link between the processes used and the resulting bodily changes. Even though medical science has accepted 'therapeutic touch' as a useful healing influence, they cannot explain why it works as well as it does.

Of course, just as patients have to believe a placebo is an authentic substance with the power to heal, so does a patient receiving alternative energy therapy have to believe they are receiving 'real' healing energies for the process to be effective. If the patient understands it's all a bluff, the healing process gets short-circuited and fails.

Medical researchers have found that the best way to prevent any subjects from knowing they're getting a placebo is to tell all research staff they are working with the "real thing," and they should handle it with care. By doing so, the beliefs of those dispensing pills will be transferred to the subjects.

However, if the patient understands the healing power of belief itself, then dramatic and lasting results are still possible even when the patient knows they are getting a placebo.

The bottom line is that it's the results which matter and not how those results are produced. If working with acupuncture, affirmations, chakras, crystals, meridian points, prescription drugs, Reiki, or pyramids will activate a patient's belief in health and healing, then by all means use whatever works.

## "It only works if you believe in it."

How many times have we heard this statement? In most cases, it's said in a derogatory way to suggest that the thing in question has no power of it's own and has to depend on the power of faith. Yet, doesn't this also suggest that the power of faith can make things work that wouldn't otherwise? What if we change it to say, "If you believe in it, it will work."?

One of the most frequent examples of this relates to the traditions of primitive religions, such as shamanism, Wicca (also known as witchcraft), or Voodoo.

You've most likely heard stories where a person has experienced a series of unlucky events and suspected they were cursed. They go to a folk-magic practitioner, who proceeds to draw strange symbols on the ground and make dramatic gestures while chanting an unknown language. All of a sudden, the curse has been lifted and the client rests a little easier knowing things will return to normal.  Sure enough, the string of unlucky events seems to have stopped and the following days are remarkably uneventful.

Many people wonder if this may be the product of coincidence, or if the connection between the ritual and results is only in our imagination.  Those who allow themselves to believe in the magic rituals will swear by the power of that magic, since they see the connection on a regular basis.  And besides, coincidence can only explain so much.  After a while, you have to accept that there's something more going on, especially when a clear pattern presents itself.

Once more, the psychologists' standard claim that this is the result of delusional thinking must be put to the test before it can be accepted.  Especially since the psychologists' theories cannot account for everything that happens in the world.

I'm willing to keep an open mind either way.  Are you?

## *Superstitions*

Have you ever known someone to carry a rabbit's foot believing it gave them "good luck"?  Maybe the foot wasn't as lucky for the rabbit, but then again, how do we know?  Maybe that particular rabbit lived a long and hoppy (er, happy) life.  What about four-leaf clovers?  You won't find too many of them in any given clover field, and their very rarity seems to give them a special significance.  Other beliefs can be found regarding the effect that breaking a mirror or walking under a ladder can have on your luck.

These traditions aren't consistent around the world.  Take the tradition of hanging a horseshoe on a door for example.  In some places, it needs to be hung with the ends pointing upward, and in other places, the ends need to point down.  In still other places, it doesn't matter which way the points face as long as the shoe itself can be touched.

Superstitions are not limited to traditional folk beliefs passed down from generation to generation. We've all heard stories about modern sports fanatics who wear their "lucky shirt" to every game to maintain a winning streak. And if it isn't a piece of clothing associated with winning, maybe it's an action they do (or don't do) before a game.

We can understand why some people believe the old superstitions because they've been handed down through the generations, but where do superstitions come from in the first place? Someone had to be the first to believe there was a connection between things like a rabbit's foot and good luck.

To answer this question, we have to understand something about ourselves. You see, our brains are wired to make connections between things — it's how we learn. Our ability to learn and adapt gave us an advantage over the other animals of the jungle, allowing us to create tools to help us do things better. However, it also predisposes us to make connections without any logical reason behind them.

A perfect example is an experience I'm having as I write this chapter. My laptop computer has developed a problem and frequently stalls during the startup process. To learn what the problem could be, I've tried several things, most of which hasn't changed it's startup behavior. At one time, I thought I found a clue when it seemed to start normally whenever I unplugged the network cable. After failing to start properly ten times in a row, I unplugged the network cable and my computer suddenly started right up. Plug the cable back in and it failed. Unplug the cable and it worked. Yep, that must have been the problem.

The next time I turned my laptop on, I forgot about the cable and left it plugged in. My computer failed to start properly. I unplugged the cable and it started up fine. Confirmation again that I was right, despite there not being any apparent reason for it.

This morning, however, I unplugged the cable before I turned on my laptop and it failed to start up. Again and again I tried, but to no avail. The network cable was NOT the problem. But for a while, I began to believe it was.

Situations like this help us understand how superstitions get started. Someone notices that they have some minor accident after walking under a ladder. If it happens enough times, a belief is formed — walking under a ladder is 'bad luck'. Then they share their insight with others and those who hear this start to wonder if it might happen to them, and the belief starts to spread like a virus and become a superstition.

Those who believe in these things can usually recite a litany of examples where their belief was proven to be true, either by their own experiences, or by the experiences of others.

Most of us have at least one thing we do because it seems to work even though there isn't any rational reason for it. Of course, if beliefs DO create our experiences, then the only logic required is that it works for us.

## *Religious Beliefs*

According to some scientists, religions are a form of superstition. But then again, some scientists believe that consciousness itself is an illusion and everything can be explained by interactions between chemicals and particles.

On one level, religion *may* have developed in the same way superstitions developed. Once you make the assumption that there is an invisible connection between one thing and another, it opens a whole new world of possibilities.

After making enough such assumptions, primitive mankind could easily have surmised that there was a spiritual being controlling life on Earth. With no idea of what such a spiritual being might have been like, it was natural to imagine God to be some sort of super-human being who could be pleased or angered.

In ancient times, stories were the primary entertainment available. At night, after a long day of hunting and gathering berries, it felt good to sit back and listen to stories explaining how the world worked and where we fit into it. The essence of good storytelling hasn't changed much, and the best stories are those with some basis in truth, making them even more believable.

When someone had a good day hunting, or narrowly escaped a saber-tooth tiger, a story about how they were aided by God gave the experience added depth and meaning. On the contrary, stories about how God punished those who disobeyed the leaders' wishes gave those leaders extra authority.

As stories were shared, they became more involved and complex, picking up new details as time progressed. Eventually people wondered how much of them were true.

Different cultures shared different stories, which accounts for the many different religions developed throughout history. Each religion offers something of value to those who practice it. They offer us a way of thinking about the "ultimate nature of the universe" in a way that is more personal and more satisfying to us.

Religion is best defined as your personal relationship with the universe. As such, each of us has our own religion, although it may share many similarities with the religions of others. We may say the same prayers to the same God and still have our own personal relationship to that God.

Some people feel more comfortable relating to a universe of matter and energy, while others are more comfortable relating to a conscious and spiritual universe. Some feel comfortable in a relationship with strict guidelines, while others are more comfortable in a relationship that's more open and loving. Some prefer the idea of a father figure ruling the universe, whereas others prefer a mother image nurturing them.

That's why there will never be "One True Religion." Different folks relate to the universe in different ways. As I see it, if God created so much variety in trees, birds, and people, God certainly must have also created variety in religion too.

## Ritual Magick

Just as some people feel more comfortable relating to a universe managed by a God with human traits, plans, and a personality, others like to relate to the universe as a system of energies and Powers that can be directed and controlled through clearly defined processes. These people are comfortable taking responsibility for *everything* in their lives.

Among the many different stories developed over time, one theme concerns itself with various rituals that may be used to direct and control spiritual energies for the attainment of specific goals, such as increased prosperity or winning the love and affection of a particular individual.

These rituals are generally grouped together into a subject called 'magick'. The 'k' on the end differentiates it from the "sleight of hand" type of stage magic, which is nothing more than an illusion.

To be successful, practitioners of ritual magick have to develop a wide set of beliefs, including the superiority of spiritual energies over physical matter, their ability to direct and control spiritual energies, and a belief in success in general. Developing the many supporting beliefs takes time and a high degree of mental concentration.

## Hypnosis

Hypnosis is a process of changing beliefs where both client and practitioner understand what is happening. Both know that the client's mind has the power to create real and lasting change within the client's body, and hypnosis is seen as a direct means of activating the mind's power.

Guiding the client into a hypnotic state is itself based on suggestion and belief. If the client believes that staring at a bright light will cause him or her to go into hypnosis, it will. And if the client believes they can be 'put under' by staring deep into the hypnotist's eyes, then it will happen exactly as they expect. Alternatively, if the client believes the hypnotist will fail, that belief also bears fruit.

A good hypnotist leverages natural responses in the induction process. By asking a client to focus on his or her breathing, the hypnotist can follow with a suggestion that the client will find themselves relaxing more and more. Since we normally relax anytime we focus on an internal process like breathing, the client subconsciously connects the response to the suggestion and gains a measure of belief in the hypnotist and the induction process.

Once the client has a solid belief in the hypnotist and the session itself, there are many techniques the hypnotist may use to access the subconscious mind directly, where most of our beliefs reside.

One such technique, which has gained a measure of popularity in recent years, is the use of the "ideomotor effect," a muscular response to a subconscious thought. Traditionally, this effect has been used in such devices as the Ouija board, pendulum divination, and dowsing. Hypnotists use this same effect to produce phenomena such as hand levitation, catalepsy (muscle rigidity), and deep physical relaxation. They also use this effect for communicating with the client's subconscious mind using unconscious movements such as eye blinks or finger twitches.

In it's currently popular form, the ideomotor effect is used in "applied kinesiology," a controversial practice involving muscle testing to communicate with a subject's subconscious mind. Supposedly, a person's muscles are weaker in the presence of harmful substances or thoughts and stronger when in the presence of more beneficial substances or thoughts. Most practitioners of applied kinesiology refute the claim that they are using hypnosis despite the obvious connection.

Whichever technique a hypnotist may use to help a client change his or her belief system, the process is generally one of direct communication with the client's subconscious mind. Through the ideomotor effect and verbal response, the hypnotist is able to gain information about the client's current beliefs, and may change those beliefs to more empowering ones with direct suggestion.

Some hypnotists are able to help their clients produce astounding cures, while other hypnotists use exactly the same procedures with the very same clients and fail miserably. The difference comes down to the client's beliefs in the two hypnotists. These beliefs are usually the result of each hypnotist's ability to match the client's pre-existing expectations, and his or her ability to formulate suggestions that integrate well with the client's other beliefs.

Hypnosis can be used to alter any belief you may have, and does so very directly. Some people are very comfortable with this directness, while others prefer to change their beliefs in a more playful manner.

# Chapter 3:  Why Isn't It Obvious?

The idea that we have the power to control every aspect of our lives simply by choosing what we believe is a very seductive concept.  However, this seems to fly in the face of common sense and traditional science.  And if it's true, then why isn't it obvious?

That's certainly a reasonable question to ask.  After all, over the course of time, we've discovered how to do many different things, including how to harness the power of the atom for both destruction and electrical power, and how to create super-complex computer systems that can produce fantastically realistic special effects in movies and television commercials.

Although when we sit and think about it, how much of what we've learned over time *was* obvious?  For example, how obvious is it to mix flour, oil, eggs, milk, sugar, baking powder, and cocoa to make a chocolate cake?  Maybe we should ask any of the thousands who have trouble getting it right *even with a recipe*.

It has always amazed me to wonder how anyone thought to mix that combination of ingredients, and to keep trying the many possible combinations until they produced an edible result.  How many eggs should we put in, one, two, twenty?  How much flour this time, a handful or a pound?

Similarly, how obvious is it to turn grapes into wine?  As I understand it, the fermentation process involves a precise control of temperature, a mix of different kinds of yeast, a way to prevent oxygen from getting to the mixture, and then waiting for 10 to 30 days.  And then there's an additional aging process after that!

Maybe we've been too busy discovering so many different things that we just haven't come around to discovering the connection between beliefs and experience.

On the other hand, even though it may not be obvious that our beliefs directly affect the world around us, there have been people throughout history who have discovered the truth and tried to tell us how important our beliefs are.  It's not exactly a new concept, but one that has been around for thousands of years.

## *Contradictory Evidence*

The problem most people have when presented with this idea is that they remember a time (or many times) when they sincerely believed something would happen and then it didn't. Or they had some other experience that contradicted one or more of their beliefs.

Maybe they went for a job interview and really believed they would get the job. But, for one reason or another, the interview didn't go well, and they were not selected for the position. Or maybe they believed that a particular individual would be attracted to them and fall in love, but events followed a different path. Whatever the situation, they remember a time when they believed one thing would happen, and yet something different transpired.

If our beliefs really do determine the experiences we have in life, then how can we possibly believe one thing and experience something different?

Let me ask you a question. When you go into a situation, do you have only one belief about it, or are there several different beliefs on several different levels relating to the same situation? Surely, if you are honest with yourself, you will realize that you have many different beliefs about any situation you encounter, and some beliefs simply contradict other beliefs.

For instance, let's say that you're starting a new relationship with someone and the two of you have gone out on a few dates. You might believe you are compatible with each other and the other person is falling in love with you. What other beliefs could influence the situation?

Do you believe you are lovable? Do you believe relationships are easy, or do you believe they are difficult? Do you believe you deserve love and happiness? Do you believe that other people are predictable, or do you believe they can do foolish things? Do you believe you generally get what you want, or do you believe you are 'unlucky'? Do you believe you always get what you expect, or do you believe that life is full of surprises?

That last question is a very powerful one. If you believe life is full of surprises and that you don't always get what you expect, can you imagine what possibilities present themselves? If beliefs control our lives, then wouldn't the belief that "we don't always get what we expect" open the door to experiencing things other than what we believe on the surface level?

The first thing we notice when we take a look at the many different beliefs affecting any one situation is the sheer number of beliefs we have within us. We take most of them for granted, believing "that's just the way it is" without realizing that our attitude about those beliefs is ITSELF a belief.

For thousands of years, scientists thought they knew that physical matter was static and infinitely predictable, and yet with the new discoveries of quantum physics, they've had to face the idea that it was only a belief, and reality could, in fact, be quite different. There's really no way of knowing what the real limits of reality might be.

This tendency to accept some beliefs as 'truths' is part of what makes us intelligent and helps us learn new things. If we had to continually question the reality of what we learned before, we'd have very little time for new discoveries. Yet, there are times when it become necessary to re-evaluate what we think we know in order to make sense of new information.

Among the many different beliefs we have within us, there are bound to be some beliefs that contradict other beliefs. For instance, at one time I believed I could do any job well, yet I also believed I would have difficulty earning money. Sometimes I believed I would never be rich, but other times believed I was destined for wealth. I believed I was special and could do more than the average person, yet I also believed success was out of my reach.

I was like the rope in a game of 'tug of war', and my beliefs were choosing sides and pulling against each other, trying to see which side was stronger. Like any real game of 'tug of war', the more players you have on your side, the easier it is to win. When you have more beliefs pulling you towards success than towards failure, you can sit back and go along for the ride.

Of course, in a game of 'tug of war', if you have a few strong players, you can still win even when the other team has more on their side. It's no great surprise to find that some beliefs are stronger than other beliefs.

## *Belief Hierarchy*

When choosing teammates for a game of strength, it's easy to decide who to pick because the ones with the biggest muscles will usually be the strongest. When looking for the strongest beliefs within your mind, what do you look for?

If you were to write out all your different beliefs about different things, you'd start to notice a pattern. Some beliefs are about what CAN be true, and other beliefs are about what CANNOT be true. Some beliefs define what is 'normal' and what can be expected in various situations. Some beliefs are about individual situations and other beliefs are about all similar situations as a group. Some beliefs are about objective reality and other beliefs are personal opinions and values.

Before we can determine which beliefs are stronger than others, we need a system to describe them. Starting with the patterns we noticed among our beliefs, we can create a belief classification system. To make it easier, we can use an existing system as a model.

One possible model is the scientific classification system for different forms of life. At the top level, we define whether a life form is a plant or animal. Within the animal category, we have subgroups like mammals, reptiles, fish, and so on. Within each of those groups, we have other, more specialized, subgroups such as *homo sapiens*. Eventually, on the bottom level, we have specific animals, including you and me. In this system, each level defines more specific groups of animals (or plants) than the level above it.

If we organize our beliefs into a similar structure, the top level would contain very general beliefs that affect every aspect of life, including answers to questions like "Is there a God?", "Do we have a soul?", and "What is the meaning of Life?" Our beliefs about the laws of science and math would also fit in here, such as our belief in gravity and our belief that 2+2=4.

The next level down would include our beliefs about the world in general. This category would contain beliefs such as "Are people basically honest and trustworthy?", "Will there ever be world harmony?", and "What's the secret to wealth?"

Moving to the next level of specificity, we have a category of beliefs about ourselves in general. Pop psychology has called this collection of beliefs our 'self-image', and here we find beliefs such as "Am I lucky or unlucky?", "Am I outgoing or shy?", "What are my relationships like?", and "Can I play a musical instrument?"

On the same level as our self-image, we would also place our beliefs about the image we have of other individuals, such as our friend David, or our cousin Suzie. Questions that reveal these beliefs include "Is this person trustworthy?", "Is this person intelligent?", "Is this person fun to be around?", and "Do I like this person?"

The more specific beliefs can be grouped together for convenience, although there are many more levels we *could* add to this classification structure. On this last level are beliefs we have about a specific job interview, or what we expect from our friend Bob when we meet with him next Tuesday, or why Mary left the party early last night.

Now that we have a system to classify beliefs, how can we use it to identify strong beliefs? And can we use it in other ways?

Just as the various theories and models of quantum physics help scientists visualize things they cannot see, the classification model we've just created can help us understand our beliefs on a more intuitive level.

The main difference between the four levels we've created is the specificity of the beliefs categorized. On the top level we have universal beliefs, followed by beliefs about the world in general, followed by beliefs about ourselves (or other individuals) in general, and finally beliefs about specific situations, events, and things. Here's a chart for easy reference:

| Belief Level | Contains |
|---|---|
| Universal Beliefs | Beliefs about universal constants such as God, karma, math, science, etc. |
| World Beliefs | Beliefs about the world in general, especially groups of people. |
| Self-Image Beliefs | Beliefs about ourselves (or others) in general and how we fit into the world. |
| Surface Beliefs | Beliefs about specific situations, events, and things. |

If you think about how a national department store chain is organized, you have the head (national) office, which sets overall operating policy, then you have regional offices responsible for groups of stores, followed by individual store managers who coordinate the departments within the store, and finally department managers who serve their customers the best they can within the bounds set by senior management.

Most customers see only the individual department managers within a store, yet everything they experience in that store is defined by policies set by upper-level management. If a customer has a problem needing to be resolved, they are usually directed first to the responsible department manager, not to the company CEO.

When a department manager seeks to resolve a customer complaint, they may propose a solution that satisfies the customer. Depending on the situation, the department manager may need to get approval for the proposed solution, so they take it to the store manager.

The store manager may approve the proposal exactly as offered, or he or she may see a need to revise it to maintain harmony with other departments within the store. In some cases, the store manager may need to seek approval from the regional office.

When the regional office is presented with a proposed solution to a customer complaint, they also have the authority to approve, deny, or modify the request. And again, in some cases the proposal may need further approval from the head office.

Once a proposal reaches the head office, there is nowhere else to go, and for the final time it gets approved, modified, or rejected. If approved or modified, it goes back down the ladder until it reaches the customer, who may or may not recognize the proposed solution as the one originally offered by the department manager.

If we use the same analogy to understand how our beliefs interact with each other, we see that a surface belief about getting a particular job may be modified or rejected by a higher-level belief, such as one that says we generally get our hopes dashed when we get too confident.

If the multi-level management analogy works, then it is safe to assume that the most powerful beliefs are the ones that set overall policy for the whole organization. As in a national department store chain, when we set policy on the top level, it filters down into all other levels automatically.

This means that when we want to change the way our beliefs create our experiences, we should focus the majority of our attention on the upper-level beliefs, and only modify more specific beliefs when necessary.

Not only does this help us identify the most important beliefs to have on our side, it also helps us make changes faster, since we only have to work on the critical 20% of our beliefs responsible for 80% of our experiences.

## *The Final Obstacle*

The most persistent obstacle to accepting that our beliefs direct the course of events in our lives is the common thought of the physical universe as an objective reality independent of our consciousness. How can anything that happens within our minds possibly affect the world around us?

Even though mystics and intuitive types have been telling us for thousands of years that the physical world is an illusion and nothing but an objectified dream, and quantum physics research is showing evidence that this may, in fact, be the case, how can we accept the idea that our thoughts can, in some way, interact with physical reality?

Let's take a moment and look at this from another viewpoint. Can you remember at least one dream you've had? You will most likely remember having many dreams, and with a little thought can recall a few of them.

Can you recall at least one dream where you ran into a wall, or stubbed your toe within the dream? It hurt, didn't it? Your experience was just as real as if it had happened in the 'real world'. Why is that? The wall wasn't actually real, but only a figment of your imagination.

Despite the many wild and crazy dreams we all have from time to time, where we fly over the landscape or walk through walls, the vast majority of our dreams follow the same patterns that exist in the physical world. The laws of physics apply just as much to the dream world as they do to the physical world, with very few exceptions.

If we fall into a lake during a dream, we get wet. If we throw something into the air, it falls down. If we spin in circles, we get dizzy. And if we have a romantic encounter, it feels equally as good as it would in the physical realm. It's as if the experiences we have in either the physical world or the dream world are created using the same set of rules.

Furthermore, when we are in a dream, not only does the dream seem to be real, but our 'real life' seems to be a dream. That is, if we have any sense of it at all. It's almost as if we live multiple lives, and each time we enter a new dream, we enter a new reality.

When we try to find the reason for this, the only sensible conclusion is that dream walls appear to be solid because we expect them to be. We become so accustomed to the way things are in real life, we carry those same beliefs into our dream lives, and those beliefs create the various experiences we dream about.

What if the same thing is happening in the physical world? What if the only reason we can't walk through walls is because we believe we can't? What if the only reason we stay on the ground is because we believe in gravity? And what if the only reason we have different types of experiences in our dream lives is because we believe we can?

The miracles produced by Sathya Sai Baba (discussed in Chapter 2) suggest that maybe we CAN do some of these things in the physical world. The many experiments in psychokinesis (mind over matter) further demonstrate that we have the capability to manipulate physical matter with our thoughts, as long as we believe it's possible.

We only have to choose to believe.

## The Universe Always Supports You

The bottom line is that you always experience the results of your beliefs. Whatever you believe, the universe will prove you right. This is incredibly powerful, but also makes the connection difficult to realize. In many respects, it resembles the age-old question, "Which came first, the chicken or the egg?" Now we wonder, "Which came first, belief or reality?"

If you believe the universe is predictable and nothing "out of the ordinary" happens, your experiences will tend to prove you right. If you believe that life is full of surprises and you don't always get what you expect, the universe will reflect your belief back to you, creating experiences to prove it. And if you believe that other people will do whatever they can to make life difficult for you, they will.

On the other hand, if you believe you're lucky and generally get everything you want, you'll have many experiences supporting your belief. If you believe money is easy to come by, you'll always have plenty of money. If you believe that people enjoy being with you, you'll find lots of evidence to prove it. And if you believe you can materialize objects out of thin air (and if your belief hierarchy also supports this belief), you'll never have to worry about food or money.

The main point to keep in mind is that we have many different beliefs, and, like the multi-level management example, higher-level beliefs can nullify or change the results that more specific beliefs would produce on their own.

It's not enough to believe you can fly. You also have to believe that the laws of physics are not absolute, that the physical world is no different from the dream world, and that flying is a normal thing to be experienced. I'm sure there are many other beliefs that also need to be in place before you can fly, so be safe and always have a net under you until you get it right, okay?

## *Summary*

These first few chapters have demonstrated the sheer power our beliefs have in our lives. We've seen some of the extreme possibilities documented by science, including phenomena such as faith healing, mind over matter, and creating objects out of 'thin air'. We've explored scientific evidence, ancient mystical teachings, and common, everyday experiences; all of them support the idea that our beliefs influence our world.

We've seen how the placebo effect extends beyond traditional medical research into all areas of life, including energy healing therapies, superstitions, and religion. We've hypothesized (made an educated guess) about the possibility that everything we experience in life may be the result of our beliefs, including the apparent solidity of walls and our experience of gravity.

While this concept may not be obvious, it isn't necessarily any less obvious than baking a cake or making wine, processes that have been used for thousands of years. The only reason we don't already take this for granted is because science has yet to give it adequate attention and study. With enough formal experimentation, we can be just as sure about this as we are about any other natural force in the universe.

Whether or not the universe has an objective reality outside of ourselves doesn't really matter. The end results are what count — what can we experience and how can we create those experiences in our lives? It's like driving a car; you don't need to understand how the engine works. As long as you know how to start it up and go, you're okay.

For several hundred years, the old model of the universe served very well, even though we now know it was inaccurate. Atoms are not discrete particles interacting with each other as we once thought, yet that model did work as if it were true.

Electricians were taught that electricity flowed through wire like water flows through a hose. It was a way of thinking about something that wasn't completely understood. Despite our almost total dependence on electricity, few of us really know what it is or how it works.

The same can be said about most of the things we use in our lives. Few photographers know how their camera works. There's probably no one in the world today who knows everything about how a computer works. And no one knows how our own minds work! Does that stop us from using them? Not usually.

All we really need to know is that something DOES work and how to use it to produce the results we want.

By using a model similar to a multi-level management structure in modern department store chains, we can understand the interactions between the many different beliefs we have within us, and how our experiences might appear to contradict our surface beliefs while conforming with our more influential universal beliefs.

Every way we look at it, it's clear that there is a direct connection between our beliefs and the experiences we have in life. It's like the direct connection between the steering wheel of a car and the path the car follows. The car's engine and other systems do the heavy work, all you have to do is push the gas pedal and turn the steering wheel.

So let's get started with the 'driving lessons' we need to take control over the path of our lives, okay?

# Chapter 4:  Discover What You Really Believe

The first step to making any real change is to first define what needs to be changed.  Before we start changing beliefs to produce a better life, we need to know what beliefs are producing the life you have now.

Many people are surprised to discover what they really believe on a deep, inner level.  We're very familiar with our surface beliefs, however, our inner, core beliefs can be significantly different.  In some cases, our inner beliefs are darker and uglier than we care to admit, so we generally ignore them and pretend we believe something prettier.

It isn't all bad in there, though.  Quite often, we find that a person believes in greater possibilities than they allow themselves to experience.  Even though higher-level beliefs are more powerful, they can still be defeated by a swarm of lilliputian beliefs.  It's quite possible you're a caterpillar about to discover your inner butterfly.

In almost all cases, we find that our inner beliefs were picked up seemingly at random, without any planning or conscious choice.  We find that sometimes we believe one thing, while other times we believe something completely different.  This contradiction usually occurs when beliefs are associated with situations or emotional feelings.  For example, when we feel good, we believe in success, but when we feel bad, we believe in failure.  Although we don't have to be concerned with these connections, knowing they happen makes it easier to understand why the contradictory beliefs exist.

As you discover what you really believe, consider this the 'before' picture to be compared with the 'after' picture when you've reached your goals.  There's no judgment about what you believe.  No 'good' or 'bad' beliefs.  The only judgment here is your own — which beliefs support the experiences you want, and which beliefs stand in your way.

Also keep in mind that the process of changing beliefs can be quick and easy. If you find a belief currently preventing you from enjoying life to the fullest, it can be a relatively small matter to change that belief into something better.

You may want to work with this belief first — your ability to change beliefs. If you believe it will be hard to change a belief, it will be. However, if you believe it will be easy, you'll have a lot more fun. If a belief looks like an angry bear, imagine it as a cute little bunny instead.

## *Discovery Process*

Discovering what you believe involves asking yourself questions. Not just any questions, but specific questions. It's not enough to ask yourself, "What do I believe about the world in general?" The questions eliciting the most accurate answers look more like "Do I believe the sky is blue?" This type of question elicits a more immediate answer that can actually be measured. Regardless of any words that spring forth, there will be an equivalent feeling elicited by the question. The strength of that feeling indicates the strength of the belief.

For instance, most people respond to a question like "Do you believe the sky is blue?" with an answer like "Yes, of course!" This shows that we believe the answer couldn't be anything other than 'yes'. On the opposite end, we have questions like "Do you believe you are living on planet Mars?" that usually produce answers like "Of course not!"

Questions producing these types of responses are special and help to calibrate a scale with which we can accurately measure our other beliefs. You can imagine your belief scale as a bathroom scale, a postal scale, a thermometer, or as a scale normally used to measure volumes, tones, pressures, or anything else you can imagine.  The only thing your scale needs is a way to record the measurement.

When we ask ourselves questions about our beliefs, we feel a level of confidence in the answer.  By choosing to assign a number to the strength of a belief, we are measuring how confident we are in it.  It's like weather predictions.  When they say there's a 60% chance of rain, they're indicating how confident they are in their belief that it will rain.

At the same time, they're also saying there's a 40% chance it won't rain.  This shows us something very important.  Any time we have a partial belief in one thing, we also have a partial belief in it's opposite.  An 80% belief in success also includes a 20% belief in failure, and a 90% belief in failure also includes a 10% belief in success.

Just as a weather prediction is for one area only, this splitting of belief is for only one 'area' at a time.  We usually have different beliefs in different situations, and the numbers may be different in each situation.  This is because many beliefs are context dependent, and each situation represents a different context.

This splitting of belief between opposites is a lot like the sand in an hourglass.  At any point in time, 100% of the sand is within the glass.  Sometimes part of the sand is on one side of the glass and the rest is in the other side.  No matter which side the sand is in, we can get all of it to the other side.  It just takes a little time.

When you think about it, belief is very much the same as the sand in an hourglass.  There's no way to increase the amount of belief you have.  It's just a matter of where your belief is placed — in success or in failure, in harmony or in discord, in health or in sickness.

Now that we have an understanding of the discovery process, let's begin by calibrating a scale with which we will measure the strength of our beliefs.  We'll do this by asking ourselves a series of questions that should produce the "of course" feeling on both ends of the scale.

I generally use a scale of 0 to 100, with 0 being the "absolutely not" end and 100 being the "absolutely yes" end. Some people use a 0 to 10 scale, and use fractions of a point, like 6.3 or 8.7. Use whichever one feels right for you.

You don't need to visualize a scale within your mind, although some people find it helpful. If you currently believe visualizing is difficult for you, and also believe that doing so will help, you may want to spend a few minutes developing your visualization skills. Start by looking at a physical scale and then imagine it with your eyes closed. After looking at the scale with your eyes open, then closed, then open, then closed again for several cycles, you'll eventually get to the point where you can see the scale as clearly with your eyes closed as you do with your eyes open.

What's important is that you select a number representing the strength of each belief as we go through the process. For this first set of questions, the only numbers that should be recorded are 0 or 100 (or 10 if you're using that scale).

## *Calibration Questions*

1. Do you believe that the sky is blue?
2. Do you believe that 2+2=4?
3. Do you believe that you are alive?
4. Do you believe that you live on planet Earth?
5. Do you believe that you live on planet Mars?
6. Do you believe that you are a human being?
7. Do you believe that you know your own name?
8. Do you believe that there are 12 seasons in a year?
9. Do you believe that the sun will rise again tomorrow?
10. Do you believe that the Earth circles the moon?

For most people, the above questions produce 7 strong 'yes' answers and 3 strong 'no' answers. This is enough to calibrate a scale for measuring the strength of other beliefs.

## *Questions To Reveal Surface Beliefs*

When digging in the ground, we have to start at the surface and work our way down. In a similar fashion, when digging through our beliefs, we start at the surface because these beliefs are easier to access. Once the soil of your mind has been tilled with these questions, and you have some experience measuring your beliefs, you'll have an easier time uncovering the deeper beliefs hidden below.

Although deeper beliefs generally have more power and deserve most of our attention, all beliefs are important. Sometimes tiny adjustments produce amazing results.

In coaching sessions, we ask very specific questions relating to each client's life and goals, however, in a book the questions have to be more general. We'll cover the areas most people want to improve, which are money, relationships, and health.

## *Money Beliefs*

1.  Do you believe that you earn enough money?
2.  Do you believe that money is hard to acquire?
3.  Do you believe that you have to work to earn money?
4.  Do you believe that one good idea can make you rich?
5.  Do you believe that only dishonest people get rich?
6.  Do you believe that the world's money supply is controlled by a small percentage of the population?
7.  Do you believe that wealth is a measure of a person's contribution to society?
8.  Do you believe that having abundant prosperity is normal and not any big deal?
9.  Do you believe that you are worth at least $1 million?
10. Do you believe that you will receive $1 million this year?

Rate your level of belief for each of the above questions before reading further. Remember to use a scale where 0 means 'absolutely not' and 100 (or 10) means 'absolutely yes'. You may want to keep track of the results for future reference by writing your answers into a notebook. This way, you'll know how much you've changed over time.

You may also find it interesting to record your level of belief in the opposite statements. If you thought of a particular situation when measuring your primary belief, think of the same situation when measuring the opposite belief. When you do this, you'll notice that the two numbers add up to something very close to 100, indicating how your belief is split between the two sides.

After reading the comments below, you'll find that some of your beliefs will change, so you may want to come back and go through the questions again. This will demonstrate very dramatically how quickly beliefs can change when exposed to a new viewpoint.

1.   <u>Do you believe that you earn enough money?</u>

We all have an 'internal thermostat' regulating the 'financial heat' in the house of our lives. It's set to what we consider 'normal'. For some people, $5000 a year is enough money, whereas for others $100,000 is not. Those who believe they earn enough money are receiving *at least as much* as the setting of their 'financial thermostat'.

What surprises most people is how this creates a contradiction between so-called 'positive thinking' and positive results. A 'positive thinker' will usually consider whatever money they receive to be enough, even when they have trouble paying their bills each month. A 'negative thinker' who complains about not having enough money has a belief that says 'normal' is more than they currently have. This belief about what is 'normal' has a great deal to do with how much money you earn, and usually causes the negative thinker to earn more money.

2.   Do you believe that money is hard to acquire?

The result of this belief is pretty obvious, wouldn't you say? If you believe that money is hard to come by, you won't have as much as you would if you believe that money comes easily. Supporting the "money is hard to come by" belief is either a belief in a limited money supply, or a belief in a relationship between work and money.  If you believe that you have to work for money, you'll repel opportunities for lucky breaks and financial leverage.

Some people never work a day in their lives, yet are considered 'rich'.  They inherit money, marry someone with lots of money, or stumble upon an idea and sell it to a multi-billion dollar company.  There are lots of people who start a new career and do better than others who have been working in that field for decades. For these successful people, it's not work, but a fun and profitable hobby.

3.   Do you believe that you have to work to earn money?

Tied very closely to the belief that you have to work to earn money is a belief in a time=money formula.  In a culture where the majority of us earn our incomes from the sale of time, most of us are programmed to believe that our incomes are limited by the number of hours available.  Even if you earn $1000 per hour, there are only so many hours in a week.

Time is not the only thing we can sell to the world.  When you have something else to sell, such as ideas, insights, or artistic expressions (music, paintings, sculpture, poetry, etc.), you can potentially earn far more for the time you invest in creating those things than you ever did as an employee.

On the other hand, many people enjoy working with others as an employee.  You're free to choose how you earn your money, just realize that you don't HAVE to work for it.

Can you feel your beliefs starting to shift as you read about some of the possibilities to enjoy lots of money without doing any real work?  Once you know it's possible, it's much easier to believe you can do it yourself.

4.  Do you believe that one good idea can make you rich?

Several of the beliefs we've looked at so far have a similar pattern — it takes a lot of time and energy to earn money in today's world. There are a lot of "get rich quick" scams in the world promising easy money. Somewhere in their claims, they suggest that you need only one good idea to make it big. Do you believe it?

According to Napoleon Hill, author of "*Think and Grow Rich*," Charles Schwab had the idea to organize a giant steel empire to rival Andrew Carnegie's dominion in that field. After 'selling' the idea to some of the richest people of the time, the new company was born, and the people involved instantly became $600,000,000 richer. $600 million dollars for a single idea!

A similar thing happened repeatedly in the 1980's as real estate was purchased, rezoned, and then sold again for a profit. The only change was the application of a new idea to the property. The same pattern happens daily on Wall Street, where companies are purchased, an idea applied, and sold again for a profit.

Many companies have a program where employees receive sizable rewards for making suggestions that improve the profitability of the company. Some ideas have been worth $25,000 to $1 million.

Someone got an idea to fold a piece of wire around itself to hold papers together and the paper-clip industry was born. Many products were failures in the marketplace until a new idea made them successful. Dixie Cups, 7-Up, Kleenex, Wheaties, root beer, Wrigley Gum, Cracker Jacks, Pepsi, and Gerber Baby Food were all failures until new ideas brought them back to life.

Yes, it took a little work to implement the ideas, but the rewards were based on the ideas, not the effort invested.

5.  Do you believe that only dishonest people get rich?

When you think of rich people, do you have an uneasy feeling that they had to do a lot of dishonest things to get where they are today?  This belief is supported by a deeper belief that it's not possible to succeed honestly, that somehow the world is set up in a way where honesty is punished and dishonesty rewarded.

Beliefs such as these will usually push us in one of two ways. Either we will stand by our principles and resign ourselves to poverty, or we'll choose to bend the rules a little here and there to get the results we seek. Now you have a third choice, to change what you believe and notice that many rich people *do* have strong moral characters. You can be one of them.

6.  Do you believe that the world's money supply is controlled by a small percentage of the population?

If I had a nickel for every time I heard this one.... It's easy to fall for this when the media publishes statistics claiming that 98% of the nation's wealth is held by only 3% of the population. The word 'held' is what does it to us. When we hold a cup, it's ours and no one else can use it.

Money isn't the same thing, however. Most of us use banks or credit unions to 'hold' our money — in checking accounts, savings accounts, money market accounts, or CD's. But what happens to that money when it's in your account? Does it just sit there and do nothing? Of course not! (My belief in that statement is a flat ZERO.) Your bank records the amount of money you deposited, and then proceeds to loan that same money out to someone else, to be paid back with interest. (I believe this statement 100%.)

No matter how many gazillion dollars rich people have stashed away, it's in circulation the whole time — as a home mortgage, as a construction loan, as investments in your uncle Bob's new business, and as insurance settlements. Every financial transaction simply moves a portion of currency from one account to another, like from my pocket to yours.

Super-billionaire Bill deposits his $20 million paycheck into his private bank, which loans money to Corporation XYZ, which pays Mary's salary, who pays the plumber for work done, who buys a pizza from Papa-J's Pizza, which purchases pepperoni from... and the cycle goes on and on and on each and every day.

Somewhere down the line, the same money is bound to end up in the hands of someone who had it earlier in the game, maybe even several times over the course of a year.

In real-life, practical terms, there really isn't any limit to the amount of money that any one person could have during a given year. The same billions can flow through my hands to yours, to your neighbors, and around again ad infinitum.

7.  Do you believe that wealth is a measure of a person's contribution to society?

Somewhat related to the last two questions, this one reveals your level of belief in a connection between wealth and something else, in this case, the contributions one makes to society. In some respects, it opposes the belief that only dishonest people get rich. When you believe contributions to society are rewarded with wealth, it sets up a nice pattern making a lot of people happy.

And yet, it's just another belief like any other. The downside is that it also relies upon the work=money belief, which limits your ability to receive wealth without doing a lot of work. This isn't necessarily bad, just something you should be aware of.

8.  Do you believe that having abundant prosperity is normal and not any big deal?

You'll want to rate your level of belief in this statement in two different ways. First, as a general statement about the probability of ANYONE having abundant prosperity, and second, as a specific statement about YOU having abundant prosperity.

This belief can form the basis for having fabulous wealth without having to work yourself to the bone for it. It is supported by the concept that you are able to do whatever feels good to you without having to wonder if you will be able to pay your bills or meet any other financial obligation. This belief allows you to pursue your passions in life for the sheer joy of doing what you love to do, without giving up material satisfaction.

I've had clients respond to such ideas with comments like "But isn't it wrong to want material possessions?" or "That would be cheating, wouldn't it?" These statements reveal inner beliefs placing a value or a moral limit upon what may be experienced. If such thoughts come up for you, pay close attention to them because they form the 'policy' handed down from your upper-level management.

Some of these "it's wrong to want wealth" ideas come from an incorrect interpretation of Christian scripture. In many places within the Bible, we're told that when God was pleased with someone, they were rewarded with great wealth. Wealth itself is not evil. What we are cautioned against is the LOVE of wealth to the exclusion of all else. As long as we maintain a balanced life, the Bible gives us a big 'thumbs up' to being rich.

As with most things in life, we can choose what we believe, and whatever we believe will be reflected in our experiences throughout life. Feel free to choose wealth.

9.  Do you believe that you are worth at least $1 million?

With this question, we are measuring our own self-worth. Very closely associated with the 'financial thermostat' we talked about earlier, your estimation of your value in monetary terms is directly reflected in your experience of wealth. When you can easily say "Yes, I'm worth at least $1 million!" you'll start to see much more money coming into your life.

While this may be a bit weird for some people, think about the many insurance settlements paid out year after year. Someone loses a leg and receives $250,000 as compensation. Or someone else loses their sight and receives $1,000,000 to compensate them for their loss. Would you trade places with these people? Probably not, and for good reason. However, if someone else's eyes are worth a million, aren't yours?

As you consider the value of all your different body parts (eyes, hands, arms, legs, feet, heart, kidneys, brain, etc.), you begin to realize just how valuable you really are.

On another line of thought, consider what it would take to build a computer capable of doing everything your brain can do. Computers are becoming faster and better every year, but it would still take well over $1,000,000 to build a computer to duplicate what goes on between your own two ears.

Gemstones and precious metals are valuable primarily because they are rare. If rubies or emeralds were as common as sawdust, we wouldn't pay so much for them. Now consider how rare you are. One of a kind! Out of the billions of people on this Earth, there is not another single person out there exactly like you.

No one has your particular sense of humor, nor your perspective on world issues. And no one could duplicate your unique artistic expressions. Look at Picasso — he couldn't draw a straight line to save his life, so he decided to change the rules of the game and create art that was unique, different, and at first, ridiculed. After the comments about childish techniques subsided, he came out okay, wouldn't you say?

Just because you don't do something the way the professionals do it doesn't mean that you aren't doing it better.

### 10. Do you believe that you will receive $1 million this year?

It's one thing to believe you deserve wealth, it's something else entirely to believe you'll actually get it. This is where most of us fall down. And the reason we fall down here is because we look around and don't see where the money could come from. We expect (believe) the future to resemble the past, or at least continue the same path we've been on for years. We look at how long it took to get to where we are now and assume that progress will continue at the same rate of speed.

What we don't generally consider are the vast possibilities beyond our perception. Remember my little experiment at the die-cutting shop where I simply decided how many hours I would get each week. Regardless of the amount of visible work, there were more jobs coming into the shop that none of us could see.

A very similar case was reported by Napoleon Hill in his classic, *"Think and Grow Rich."* A clergyman named Dr. Frank Gunsaulus had dreamed for years of creating a new type of school to correct what he saw to be defects in the traditional education system. He needed about a million dollars to implement his plan, and nothing much happened until one Saturday when he decided he would get the required money, and he would have it within a single week. Immediately after making the decision, he got an idea to make his school idea the focus of the next day's sermon. He called the papers to announce the title of his sermon, "*What I Would Do If I Had a Million Dollars.*"

Dr. Gunsaulus spent the rest of the day preparing his talk, and by that evening, he felt as if he were already in possession of the money. Sunday morning, he forgot his notes and had to rely on his memory. This turned out to be a blessing, as he was able to put his whole heart and soul into delivering his message.

At the end of the sermon, a man from one of the back rows slowly walked to the front. Once there, he said, "Reverend, I liked your sermon. I believe you can do everything you said you would, if you had a million dollars. To prove that I believe in you and your sermon, if you will come to my office tomorrow morning, I will give you the million dollars. My name is Phillip D. Armour."

With the money Armour gave Gunsaulus, the Armour Institute of Technology was founded, which later became the Illinois Institute of Technology.

Dr Gunsaulus received his million dollars within 36 hours of choosing to believe he would. He had the idea, someone else had the money. They needed each other.

There will always be wealthy people who need places to invest their money, as well as those who feel a need to contribute to society, freely giving money to anyone who needs it.

## *Relationship Beliefs*

1.  Do you believe that people respond well to you?
2.  Do you believe that you fit in with others?
3.  Do you believe that it takes work to keep a relationship?
4.  Do you believe that it's easy to find a compatible partner?

5. Do you believe that there are many who are looking for someone like you?
6. Do you believe that you are a lovable person?
7. Do you believe that you must hide certain aspects of yourself to be accepted?
8. Do you believe that a relationship can be a source of continuous celebration?
9. Finish the following statement: to find a great relationship, you have to _____.
10. Finish the following statement: people like me usually have _____ relationships?

As before, note down the strength of your beliefs in the above statements before reading further. This helps demonstrate the power of new information to change our beliefs and makes it easier to change other beliefs in the future. After you read the comments below, feel free to come back and measure your beliefs a second time to see how much they've changed.

1. <u>Do you believe that people respond well to you?</u>
This is another one of those "chicken or the egg" beliefs. Did the belief come before the experience, or did the experience produce the belief? Many times it's a matter of interpretation. "Respond well" means different things to different people.

What I generally find with clients who believe that others do not respond well to them is that at some point in the distant past, someone responded in a way that felt (or was misinterpreted to be) 'negative'. Most of the time, this 'negative' response happened early in life and set up an expectation of this being 'normal'. If the client later sees that others do not have the same experience, the belief changes from a world-level belief (true for everyone) to a self-image belief indicating something is 'wrong' with them as an individual.

In the next chapter, we will discuss in more detail how these types of beliefs get their start. For now, realize that in most cases, somewhere deep in our past, we may have simply misinterpreted an event, which created a tiny belief, which in turn caused us to misinterpret other events, and the process blossomed into a strong belief we assume is fact.

2.   Do you believe that you fit in with others?

   This is a self-image belief influencing all of our relationships. It's also a judgment we place upon ourselves and everyone else. How do we really know that others are happier or more confident? Maybe they're just faking it. Or coming from the other direction, how do we know that we are more intelligent or morally superior to the masses? Maybe we're just deluding ourselves.

   If we hold onto a belief that we are substantially different from the majority of people, we create a barrier that tends to keep us separate. In extreme cases, it causes us to be alone much of the time, even when we'd rather not be. It also tends to create discord between us and the people we interact with on a daily basis.

   Despite the vast amount of programming that suggests the sexes are as different as Mars and Venus (especially coming from people who cannot maintain a relationship themselves), we all have a body, a brain, a mind, an intellect, emotions, and goals. We all want to feel respected and accepted by others. We all have a tendency to avoid pain and to indulge in pleasurable activities. Those aspects of ourselves that are special and unique are just icing on the cake.

   When we choose to believe that we are pretty much the same as everyone else, it opens a doorway to smoother relationships in all areas of life.

3.   Do you believe that it takes work to keep a relationship?

   Usually the result of several previous beliefs, which were themselves the products of misinterpretation and judgment, this belief comes up in all kinds of relationships, although more often in friendships and romance. Supporting this belief are the beliefs that other people don't want what we want and that we are fundamentally different in some way.

Also involved in many cases is a hidden belief that we are not valuable enough to keep the other person's attention. This, in turn, is based on another belief that people naturally choose to be involved with the most valuable person they can.

Supporting all of this is yet another belief that we have to compromise in some areas to get what we want in other areas, or in other words, that we are unable to get everything we want. This is very closely associated with a collection of beliefs defining what is 'normal' for a relationship. When we change our concepts of what is 'normal', most of the other beliefs change as well.

4.   Do you believe that it's easy to find a compatible partner?

This belief finally turned my love-life around. For many years, I assumed I was so different that there was probably only a dozen people in the whole world I could truly be compatible with. Once I realized how this belief was limiting me, I decided to believe that there were many thousands of compatible women within my own city, and that, very likely, I'd run into several of them every day. Very shortly afterwards, I met the woman who is now my wife, and we're very happy together.

I've known a lot of people who thought that only one person in the whole world could be their 'soul mate'. Even worse, they believed there wasn't any guarantee they would ever find each other "in this lifetime." These beliefs set up an expectation that romantic relationships will rarely be entirely satisfying.

As mentioned above, this belief is supported by the belief that we are fundamentally different from other people, and so, when we change that belief, this one changes automatically.

5.   Do you believe that there are many who are looking for someone like you?

This is a companion belief to the one above. If you believe that no one wants someone like you, then that is what you'll experience. However, if you choose to believe that there are thousands who want someone *exactly* like you, then your experience will be quite different.

6.  Do you believe that you are a lovable person?

This belief is closely associated with several of the above beliefs, although focused primarily on romantic relationships. It's also important only to the extent that we believe it's important. If we believe it's not necessary to build a relationship on lovable qualities, then the belief about whether or not we are lovable loses importance. And then there is the belief about what constitutes "lovable." For some, being lovable means lots of cuddling in front of a fire or candlelit bubble-baths, whereas for others, being lovable means having lots of integrity and honor.

Whatever we believe about our 'lovability' tends to be reflected in our lives. Choose to believe that you are lovable.

7.  Do you believe that you must hide certain aspects of yourself to be accepted?

Most of us have some part of ourselves we are at least a little bit ashamed of. Maybe we've done something in the past we'd rather forget, or maybe we have a birthmark that we think is ugly. Whatever it is, some of us believe that others would reject us if they knew about it.

This belief tends to cause us to keep secrets from others, including within romantic relationships. These secrets create a separation that sometimes causes the other person to distrust us, possibly to the point of breaking off the relationship.

Once again, this belief is supported by beliefs about our value as a person, our being different from others, and the compatibility between ourselves and another person.

8.  Do you believe that a relationship can be a source of continuous celebration?

This question gets into your beliefs about what is possible within a relationship. You will almost never experience something you believe is impossible, and the degree to which you believe something is possible will determine the likelihood you will actually experience it.

This belief is based on another belief about the possibility of experiencing perfection.

9.  <u>Finish the following statement: to find a great relationship, you have to</u> _____ .
   Anywhere you find the phrase "have to," there is an underlying belief.  If you believe you "have to" do anything to find a great relationship, then you've placed limits on that experience.
   On the other hand, if you believe you don't "have to" do anything to find a great relationship, then you've opened the door to having a great relationship come into your life with no effort.

10. <u>Finish the following statement: people like me usually have</u> _____ <u>relationships?</u>
   Statements like this help to reveal our beliefs about what is normal for us.  If we believe that people like us normally have lousy relationships, guess what we'll have in our lives?  If we believe that people like us have wonderful relationships, then our relationships will be simply magnificent!
   To get to the supporting beliefs, ask yourself "Why?"  Whatever answer comes up in response to that is another belief, usually on a more powerful level.  If you keep asking yourself "Why?" for each belief that comes up, eventually you'll reach a point where the answer is "just because," and that is, most likely, a core belief.  We'll discuss this process in more detail later in this chapter.

## *Health Beliefs*

1.  Do you believe that getting sick is normal?
2.  Do you believe that the body heals itself naturally?
3.  Do you believe that your cells are constantly renewed?
4.  Do you believe that the body breaks down with age?

5. Do you believe that your DNA controls your health?
6. Do you believe that your body is a reflection of your consciousness?
7. Do you believe that miracles of healing have taken place?
8. Do you believe that miracles of healing still happen?
9. Do you believe that you could live forever?
10. Finish this phrase: to be healthy, I have to _____.

As we saw earlier, the evidence regarding the placebo effect and faith healing proves that our beliefs about health have a profound impact on our experience of health. In fact, we found that our beliefs about a treatment have a far greater effect on our health than the treatment itself.

This suggests that everything we *think* we know about germs, bacteria, viruses, and everything else could simply be a convenient model that happens to produce results, like the models used by quantum physicists which help to produce new technological advances. The models may not be entirely accurate, but as long as they work, that's what really counts.

*Science* magazine published an article in 2000 about an incident from the early days of the Germ Theory. To debunk the theory, a scientist drank a glass of water filled with the *vibrio cholerae* bacteria, which supposedly causes cholera. Surprising the theory's supporters, he did not contract the disease and remained completely symptom-free, proving the germs were innocent. Despite this, medical scientists maintain that *vibrio cholerae* causes cholera.

In more modern times, large numbers of people have been found to carry the HIV virus for decades without any symptoms of AIDS. Obviously, the virus does not cause the disease.

We've all heard similar stories, like the many people who aided those suffering during "The Plague" in Europe without any ill effects whatsoever. These stories prove that germs do not cause disease, and suggest other factors as being responsible.

To get a better understanding of how we came to believe the current model of health and healing, consider this: somewhere a long time ago, someone was the first to believe there HAD to be a physical cause for sickness and disease. That one person convinced others to believe the same thing, and eventually, those who believed this discovered viruses, bacteria, and other unseen 'causes' of illness.

In many respects, this is similar to the quantum physicists' beliefs about the existence of smaller and smaller subatomic particles, which were found soon after they were believed to exist. Whether those things pre-existed or were created through the power of belief we may never really know.

The question I put to you, dear reader, is *what if* the only reason germs exists is because we believe they do? *What if* the only reason we respond to medical treatment is because we believe that it works? And *what if* we could be completely healthy all of the time simply by choosing to believe we will?

1.  Do you believe that getting sick is normal?

You'll find that the strength of this belief will correlate very closely with the frequency with which sickness visits your home. Those who believe it's normal to get sick have weaker immune systems than those who believe that sickness is abnormal. This has the same effect as the belief that poverty is normal, or that bad relationships are the status quo.

If we believe that we can get sick at the drop of a hat, we will. However, if we believe we are always healthy, our experience is quite different. This is why many people constantly concerned with vitamins and health supplements are often more sickly than those who simply take it on faith they will be healthy.

2.  Do you believe that the body heals itself naturally?

It's easy to believe that the body heals itself when cut or bruised, and even mends bones back together when broken, but do you believe that the body heals itself no matter what the condition? Does your belief about the body's ability to heal itself extend to conditions such as cancer, tuberculosis, pneumonia, and even nearsightedness?  At what point do you start to believe that the body's healing process requires help?

The research we examined earlier in this book proves that the body can heal itself of practically ANY condition, provided you believe it can.

3.  <u>Do you believe that your cells are constantly renewed?</u>

This is something scientists have told us for years.  In fact, scientists have told us that every tissue in the body is completely replaced on a regular basis.  Our bones take the longest to replace, with estimates ranging from eleven months to ten years.  This means there is no part of your body more than ten years old!

4.  <u>Do you believe that the body breaks down with age?</u>

If there is no part of our bodies more than ten years old, then why would people grow old?  Most theories center around the concept that the renewal process isn't perfect, mistakes happen, and replacement cells are imperfectly created.

However, if that were true, then how could the human race survive as long as it has?  After all, a perfect newborn baby is created from the cells of it's parents.  If cell deterioration occurred the way they say, then a baby would be born with cells already partially deteriorated.

Since this doesn't happen, there must be a different reason for the aging process.  Our beliefs in aging, perhaps?

5.  <u>Do you believe that your DNA controls your health?</u>

Even though the Human Genome Project proved that we have far too few genes in our DNA to account for our incredible range of complexities, this belief proposed by the scientific community is persistent.  It does seem logical.  And since those scientists who believe this theory are finding connections between genes and physical traits, the idea is supported by evidence.

However, as we've found, evidence can be found to support ANY theory, so this is no longer enough to prove it to be an objective truth. Now we have to consider the effect our beliefs have on the situation.

Actually, this belief wouldn't be a problem if we also believe that our DNA is perfect and maintains optimal health. Then we'd have a good, solid reason to expect to be healthy.

Scientists had to find *some* way to explain why people are born with wildly different physical characteristics. Basing their research on the core belief that there had to be a physical reason for everything, they ignored any beliefs possibly influencing each birth (probably too many to track), and looked for something special within our cells. Their beliefs were confirmed by the discovery of a double-helix protein which seemed to carry the necessary information.

I wonder what they would have found if they based their research on the idea that reality is a reflection of our beliefs?

6.  Do you believe that your body is a reflection of your consciousness?

Or do you believe that your body is a reflection of your DNA? This is an alternative to the above belief, and one mentioned many times in popular literature over the past 100 years or so.

This belief is based on a deeper belief in the inter-connection between consciousness and physical matter. It's also based on a belief that consciousness is the guiding force behind the physical universe.

The nice thing about this belief is that it allows for profound changes taking place within moments. The potential problem with this belief is that it requires us to maintain a 'healthy' conscious-ness to maintain physical health.

7.  Do you believe that miracles of healing have taken place?

This question asks if you accept the facts documented by many people around the world. It's based on your beliefs about whether or not others can be trusted to tell the truth, and about the possibility of events not supported by modern science. Before you can experience a miraculous healing, you have to be willing to accept the possibility that such things have happened before.

8.   Do you believe that miracles of healing still happen?

I've heard preachers tell their congregations that the miracles of healing which took place during the ministry of Christ were used to prove his divinity and that they no longer occur. I've heard quite a few others express similar beliefs, as if what may have been true in times past is nothing but fantasy today.

Clearly, these folks base their belief on the idea that miracles depend on one or more factors which have changed over time. When we sit and think about how the fundamental nature of the universe (or God) could have possibly changed in the last 2000 years, nothing of any substance comes to mind.

To believe that miracles do not happen, you also have to distrust the reports made by the thousands of people who have experienced miraculous healings even in modern times. At this point, any rejection of the numerous reports of healing, both in the past and in the present, is simply a matter of personal choice.

9.   Do you believe that you could live forever?

This question tests the boundaries of what we can believe. Once we accept the fact that our cells are constantly being replaced, that there is no part of us more than ten years old, and that cell replacement does not deteriorate with time, what's left to oppose the belief that we could, in fact, live as long as we choose?

Actually, the only reason we have trouble believing this is because we don't know anyone who has lived much longer than our concept of a normal lifespan. Of course, our lack of information may be a result of our belief, so it's another catch-22 situation.

In the annals of history, there have been a few rumors of people living a great many decades without a single alteration in their physical appearance. According to biologists, several life forms appear to be immortal. Bacteria, certain types of jellyfish, and hydra (tiny water-dwelling animals) are all examples of life forms that do not experience death as we know it.

10. Finish this phrase: to be healthy, I have to _____.

Here we have another "have to" phrase which helps us discover our inner beliefs. When you follow this with the question "Why?", you have a powerful tool for revealing the foundations of your life.

## *Self-Image Beliefs*

1.  Do you believe that you are a good person?
2.  Do you believe that people generally accept you?
3.  Do you believe that you deserve to be happy?
4.  Do you believe that you have a good life?
5.  Do you believe that you are gifted in some way?
6.  Do you believe that you have a purpose in life?
7.  Do you believe that you make good choices?
8.  Do you believe that you make mistakes?
9.  Do you believe that you have more problems than others?
10. What is 'normal' for your life?

It's time to dig deeper and start asking ourselves about our self-image beliefs. This set of questions gives you some direction for discovering what you believe about yourself in general. These beliefs are more powerful than your surface beliefs, although in rare cases it's possible a surface belief could overpower a self-image belief.

As we proceed, you'll notice that some questions lead to other questions, which in turn, reveal deeper, more powerful beliefs. Go ahead and measure the strength of these newly discovered beliefs. The more you know about what you believe, the more control you have down the road. (And consider whether you believe that 'control' is good or bad.)

1.  <u>Do you believe that you are a good person?</u>
Before we can answer this question, we need to have a concept of what is 'good'.  What traits or characteristics define a 'good person'?  To what degree do these traits need to exist before a person can be considered 'good'?

Connected with this belief is the belief about what results from being a good person.  Do you believe that being good will cause you to receive more of what you want in life?  Do you believe that others will respond to you in a more satisfactory way?  Do you believe that you will be favored by God in some way?  Do you believe that you will be punished if you are not good?  All of these beliefs will influence the things you experience in life.

2.  <u>Do you believe that people generally accept you?</u>
When you meet someone for the first time, is it more likely that they will accept you, or is it more likely that they will find fault with you?  As people get to know you, do they usually enjoy being with you, or do they find excuses to be somewhere else?  If we accept the idea that our beliefs create our experiences, then somewhere along the line, a belief was created that caused these patterns to form.  Furthermore, a change in belief can result in a change of experience.

When we choose to believe that people generally accept us, we soon find that job interviews, meetings, dates, and social outings become more enjoyable.

3.  <u>Do you believe that you deserve to be happy?</u>
This question taps into a whole range of beliefs.  Beliefs about worthiness, about value and self-worth, about outcomes from various projects and goals, and about our overall 'luck'.  It's pretty easy to see how this belief affects our experiences with money, relationships, health, parenting, buying and selling a home, and everything else we do in life.

It's possible to believe a specific situation will go well, but if we also believe that we don't deserve to be happy, then the surface belief will be neutralized and we'll be disappointed.  However, if we truly believe that we deserve happiness, then we'll get many happy surprises even in the presence of negative surface beliefs.

4.  <u>Do you believe that you have a good life?</u>
Once again, we have to define what a 'good life' is before we can answer this question.  What is associated with a good life? What differences distinguish a good life from an average one?

Obviously, if you believe you have a good life, you'll likely expect good things to happen often.  And as you begin to expect better and better results from everything you do, you'll start to see more and more evidence supporting your new belief.

5.  <u>Do you believe that you are gifted in some way?</u>
With this question, we probe to find if you believe that you have any special advantages other people may not have.  This supports a belief that you will have an easier time in life than others.  The two beliefs are not necessarily related, however, as it's quite possible to believe that you are gifted, yet also believe that you will have a hard time in life.  Some people believe they are persecuted for being gifted.

Of course, we can also ask what it means to be gifted, and what the results might be.  Does being gifted automatically lead to happiness, or does it require greater responsibility?  Is it possible for both to exist together?  And is it possible to be gifted in some way, yet not realize what that gift may be?

6.  <u>Do you believe that you have a purpose in life?</u>
Those who believe they have a purpose in life generally accomplish far more than those who believe otherwise.  They also tend to believe they will find support when they need it, regardless of whether or not they see it.  Many who believe they have a purpose in life also believe they will have an easier time when actively fulfilling it

Associated with this belief are beliefs about what a life purpose may be, the defining characteristics involved, what a life purpose may require, and the potential rewards for a life well lived. Likewise, do you believe that a life purpose is something you can choose, or do you believe it was set before you were born?

7.  Do you believe that you make good choices?

When faced with a choice, are you confident that you will make a good one, or do you inwardly fear making a mistake? Just as in the psychic research labs, the more you believe in your ability to make successful choices, the more your choices will be correct. It doesn't really matter whether this means our choices will be based on 'intuition' or if our choices will directly change reality. The effect is the same.

Many times, we find that a person's expectation of making good choices is directly proportional to their belief in positive outcomes. It's almost like they believe that making a choice is a bit like flipping a coin or throwing dice.

However, when a person believes that they are a perfect choice-making machine, their success rate jumps higher than an Olympic gold medalist.

8.  Do you believe that you make mistakes?

This is very much opposite from the belief question above, worded to reflect a yes/no or true/false condition. Here's an intriguing question: what do you suppose would happen if you firmly believed you COULD NOT make mistakes? Considering the impact our beliefs have on our experiences, I'd speculate that such a belief would produce some outstanding results.

9.  Do you believe that you have more problems than others?

Some people believe they are blessed. Others believe they are cursed. To gather more information about the beliefs support-ing this one, ask yourself "Why?" This will shed additional light on the subject.

Keep in mind that we rarely know everything about other people. They may have many more problems than you know, possibly a lot more. Also, you may be discounting many pleasant events in your life.

As an experiment, keep a notebook with you for a whole week and mark down every experience as a plus, a minus, or a check-mark to indicate whether they were pleasant, disagreeable, or neutral. Track even the smallest things, such as when you get out of bed each morning, and when you talk with various people.

10. <u>What is 'normal' for your life?</u>
This question is a bit different, however, it also reveals a lot about what you believe. How would you describe what is 'normal' for you and your life? Regardless of how many facts support these beliefs, they are still beliefs, which are always reflected in the events and conditions of your life.

Measure the strength of each belief involved in your life description. Then, if you care to dig further and discover the beliefs supporting them, ask yourself "Why is this true?" for each statement you used to describe your life. This will lead you into a nest of supporting beliefs, which maintain the 'normality' of your life.

## *World Beliefs*

1. Do you believe that the world is on the brink of destruction?
2. Do you believe that the world is becoming more and more enlightened?
3. Do you believe that people like to help others?
4. Do you believe that people are interested only in themselves?
5. Do you believe that only the strong survive?
6. Do you believe that cooperation is the key to success?
7. Do you believe that cutting costs is the best way to business success?
8. Do you believe that being excellent is a better path to success?
9. Do you believe that people are generally reasonable?
10. Do you believe that people are arrogant idiots?

This set of questions helps you discover the beliefs you have about the world at large. From the comments in earlier sections, you can most likely trace the lineage of beliefs revealed here, and so I won't bore you with unnecessary details.

For most people, the above questions suggest opposite ideas. This helps make a dramatic illustration of exactly where your belief is split between the two. In certain rare cases, I've found people who honestly believed both sides simultaneously. This happens when the client sees the two ideas as being separate and distinct from each other.

I've met many people who thought they believed in a world where people live in harmony with each other, only to find they really believed that people are just out for themselves. This usually happens when someone hasn't really analyzed what they believe and simply assume that they have positive beliefs.

Sometimes it's good to imagine you're playing a game where giving the right answer will cause you to win a million dollars, and being wrong, even by a small amount, causes you to lose. Then it isn't a matter of which belief sounds better, it becomes a matter of which one feels more true.

When you're honest with yourself, you have an opportunity to make positive and lasting changes.

## *Universal Beliefs*

1. Do you believe that there is a God?
2. Do you believe that God is a judge?
3. Do you believe that God is a teacher?
4. Do you believe that God is a playmate?
5. Do you believe that God is a protector?
6. Do you believe that God answers prayers?
7. Do you believe that there is only one God?
8. Do you believe that we are all part of One Great Being?
9. Do you believe that life is a series of lessons to be learned?

10. Do you believe that life is a playground where all we have to do is have fun?
11. Do you believe that life is a jungle where only the strong survive?
12. Do you believe that we are spiritual beings having a human experience?
13. Do you believe that the universe follows strict physical laws which cannot be changed or broken?
14. Do you believe that precognition is merely coincidence?
15. Do you believe that miracles are real?
16. Do you believe that miracles are delusions?
17. Do you believe that magick is evil?
18. Do you believe in Heaven and Hell?
19. Do you believe that it's wrong to want things?
20. Do you believe that time is an illusion?
21. Do you believe that there is more to the universe than we can comprehend?

As you can easily imagine, the list above is only a small sampling of the questions we *could* ask ourselves. However, it should help you discover what you believe about the overall nature of the universe and life.

## Self-Analysis

Obviously, there are an endless variety of questions we could ask ourselves to discover what beliefs may be hiding below our surface awareness. While the questions presented in this chapter give you an excellent start, they are not intended to reveal all you may need to address.

We could actually uncover ALL our beliefs if we were to stop and ask ourselves a question about everything, but that would also impair our ability to function properly. Imagine reading a newspaper, or listening to a television program, or even speaking to a friend, and stopping to measure your belief in every statement. You wouldn't be able to do anything else!

We could stop and measure our beliefs in statements and events relating to one specific issue, such as prosperity, relationships, health, or how people respond to each other in business situations. Thus, we can analyze our beliefs about one issue in depth without too much interruption to our normal lives.

For each experience or portion of an experience, notice what brought it to your awareness. This may suggest a mental association between events and conditions. For instance, if we find ourselves getting impatient, we can ask our inner mind to reveal what aspect of the situation is causing our impatience. We can ask ourselves to remember similar situations. We can ask about our expectations of the future. We can ask about our beliefs in impatience itself. All of these questions will help reveal the intricate structure of beliefs supporting our current experience.

As we do this, it's important to remember that everything is a belief, no matter how many memories we have to support it's 'truth'. Just because we can remember 1000 times when we failed to complete a task or were rejected by someone at the final moment, that's no reason to accept it as an absolute truth. As soon as we change our beliefs relating to similar situations, our experiences will change to support the new 'truth'.

## *Belief Archeology*

Self-analysis works very well when you have lots of time. Most of us, however, would like a quicker process to discover the beliefs behind a specific issue. In these cases, we can modify the procedure to produce immediate results. How's THAT for instant gratification?

Here's an outline of the process, followed by an explanation:
1.  Define your target goal.
2.  In vivid detail, imagine yourself experiencing your goal.

3. After a few moments, ask yourself "What's stopping me from attaining this goal?"
4. Write down what feels to be correct.
5. Rewrite the answers into supporting statements.
6. For each of the new statements, ask "What's stopping this from being true?"
7. Write down what feels to be correct.
8. Continue with step 5 until the answers are something like "Just because."

1. <u>Define your target goal.</u>

Everything starts with a goal. It's like planning a vacation. Where do you want to go?  When do you want to be there?  What do you want to do when you get there?

If your goal is simply to "be happier," that's fine — just define it as much as you can. What does it feel like? How will you know when you're happier?  What signs indicate you've reached your goal?

2. <u>In vivid detail, imagine yourself experiencing your goal.</u>

Imagine yourself in a situation that's only possible after you've reached your goal.  Mentally see proof you've reached your goal. Feel the emotions you expect to feel then. Move your body like you're there. Pretend it has already happened.

3. <u>After a few moments, ask yourself "What's stopping me from attaining this goal?"</u>

While most 'creative visualization' experts suggest you take steps 1 and 2, they leave you there without taking the vital next step.  In fact, these 'experts' claim that thinking about possible obstacles will kill the process, and in so doing, reveal that they believe negative thinking is more powerful than positive thinking. Of course, the belief will produce evidence to support itself.

On a related note, we can easily see why some experts teach that positive thoughts are 1000 times more powerful than negative thoughts. What a WONDERFUL belief to have!

By asking ourselves what's stopping us from reaching our goal, we are giving ourselves an opportunity to face the challenge and win. If there's a hole in the boat, let's plug it and move on. If we ignore it, we may sink before we reach our destination. Here's one example of using negative thinking for a very positive purpose.

By bringing these limiting beliefs into our awareness, we can change them to work FOR us instead of AGAINST us.

4.  Write down what feels to be correct.

This helps us remember the limiting beliefs we've found within us. If we can change these to supporting beliefs, it's like taking a 'tug of war' player from one team and putting him or her on the opposing team.   By writing down our current beliefs, we won't forget to change any of them.

5.  Rewrite the answers into supporting statements.

In this step, we transform negative statements into positive ones. For example, if our goal is to double our income in the next year, and we find a limiting belief of "my boss won't give me a raise," then we rewrite this statement to be something like "my boss will give me a substantial raise." If we can believe this new statement, our goal will be easier to reach.

6.  For each of the new statements, ask "What's stopping this from being true?"

Continuing the example above, we ask ourselves something like "What's stopping my boss from giving me a substantial raise?" This gives us a deeper, more powerful, level of belief.

7.  Write down what feels to be correct.

As we dig down into the heart of an issue, many different beliefs will present themselves. Keep track of all of them.

8.  Continue with steps 5 through 7 until the answers are something like "Just because."

You'll know you've reached a core-level belief when the statement is assumed to be true without any justification. These beliefs are the most influential. When you change them, all beliefs depending on them automatically change as well.

If you're really ambitious, go through this process again, asking yourself positive questions to help you uncover supporting beliefs. Once uncovered, these beliefs give you extra support.

Go back to your original goal statement; for instance, doubling your income this year. Now ask yourself "What's helping me double my income this year?", or "What can I do to double my income this year?" This may reveal forgotten information, such as a reward plan the company has for employees who submit good ideas, or a business opportunity you saw on the Internet.

This will give you additional players on your team, making it easier to win. Remembering what's in your favor will give your supporting beliefs added strength and weaken the opposing beliefs. It's like the way athletes "psych out" their opponents to gain an advantage, or the way a business person uses key information during a negotiation. You can use the same strategy within your own mind very effectively.

# Chapter 5:  Choosing New Beliefs

I n this chapter, we'll take a look at various techniques we can use to reshape what we believe.  These techniques have been collected from a wide variety of sources, so you're sure to find something that resonates with you.  Some techniques are fun and playful, while others are structured and 'serious'.  Use whatever feels right for you, including a combination of techniques.

## *What Beliefs Are*

Although we've been discussing the power of belief throughout this book, we have yet to actually define what a belief is.  This will help us dig a little deeper and be more effective in our work.

According to the Merriam-Webster online dictionary, a belief is "a state or habit of mind in which trust or confidence is placed in some person or thing."

Pretty simple, actually.

Of course, to *really* understand this, we need to know exactly what it means to place trust or confidence in something or someone.  What happens inside our minds when we trust someone?  Do our minds put them into a folder of a different color, or place a sticker on their head that says "trust me"?

It's a cute image, but probably not very accurate.  It's more likely that our minds simply create an association between a person and the concept of trust itself.  Kind of like a dictionary reference that says "see also..."

Whenever our minds call up a memory, a number of associated thoughts and emotions are brought forth along with it.  That's why when you think of the concept of 'dog', you get one or more images representing what that word means.  And if you have any strong emotions about dogs in general, or even about one specific dog from your past, they will also come forward and be recognized, even if only on a subconscious level.

When you think about what it means to trust someone, your mind brings up associated memories demonstrating trust in action, and a feeling of trust and confidence comes with them, whether you consciously recognize it or not.

The same thing happens in reverse. When you think of a particular person you trust, your mind activates the associated thought of what trust itself is. And when you think about something you believe in completely, your mind brings forth a feeling of confidence along with it.

This phenomenon is the central mechanism responsible for our capacity to learn. If our minds did not recall associated memories, we would not be able to use previous knowledge to handle current circumstances. We would have to relearn everything all over again each time we encountered the same type of situation.

So every morning, we'd have to relearn how to walk, and every time we got into a car, we'd have to relearn how to drive. How would we ever get anywhere?

This phenomenon is also why our universal beliefs and our beliefs about the world in general are so much more influential than our beliefs about one specific situation. They are referenced more often.

## *Learning New Beliefs*

Since a belief is a mental association between a person or thing and the concepts of trust and confidence, and this mental process of associating things together is central to the process of learning, then it makes sense to say that we form new beliefs by *learning* them.

We learn that 2+2=4 and the Earth revolves around the Sun. Once we learn these things, we believe them. Maybe not at first, though. Our high-school math teachers tried to teach us that 21x+14y=3z too, but we had to see it for ourselves before we believed them. We first needed supporting information and proof before we accepted their word and trusted the information they gave us.

The same is true with people. We gradually grow to believe that a person is trustworthy. We don't necessarily trust them right away, unless we believe it's okay to trust new people. Most of us refrain from trusting them completely until we can identify a pattern of truthfulness. Only then do we *really* trust them. And if we ever find that what they say is in any way untrue, we mentally associate them with the concept of 'distrust' rather than 'trust' and they have to work that much harder to win us over.

Let's take a quick look at this process from the beginning to get a better idea of how it works.

As infants, we started to form our own concepts of the world. Early concepts were limited to light/dark, soft/hard, pain/pleasure, and other dualities. As our experience grew, more detailed and subtly defined concepts became possible.

At the very beginning, our minds were empty slates, upon which anything could be written. We could believe in happiness or frustration, acceptance or rejection, success or failure. With our minds open to all possibilities, the beliefs held by those around us (parents, caregivers, siblings, and neighbors) created our early experiences.

Since it's only natural to believe in what we experience, whatever we happened to experience as a result of *their* beliefs became *our* earliest beliefs. If our parents believed in loving relationships, we experienced the harmony that resulted from their beliefs and learned to expect loving relationships in our own lives. If they believed in lack and limitation, the experiences they created for us established a pattern of belief within us.

This is an important point to keep in mind. Any time we enter into a new situation where we have no preconceived beliefs, what we actually experience could very well be the product of other people's beliefs. In other words, we experience a reality created by other people.

In most cases, however, we enter into a new experience with a set of preconceptions based on past experience. Every time we encounter a new situation, we mentally search for any similarities to earlier situations. If we find any, we automatically and instantly recall our beliefs about the earlier situation(s) and temporarily associate them with the current one. Once again, this is central to how we learn.

These temporary beliefs may be weak, but they set our initial expectations in a new situation. Because our natural tendency is to interpret our experiences within the context of these expectations, our interpretations may be colored by them and lead us to create beliefs that are substantially different than if we had entered into the new situation with a different perspective.

In the process of learning, each new bit of information is first evaluated within the context of previously learned material before being accepted. This process helped us become the dominant species on the planet. It's also why our early experiences form the foundation for our personalities and set us on the course we generally take through life. Only through conscious choice, do we ever deviate from the path set by our early experiences.

Whenever new information challenges our previously learned beliefs, we first discount it. We assume it must be incorrect. If it's validity is proven, our minds then attempt to form a new belief to account for both old and new information. In many respects, this is similar to the scientific method, although it is more personal and not always logical. We hypothesize (make an educated guess) about what could explain the discrepancy, and if it "feels right," we move forward as if the hypothesis were true.

I experienced this when my laptop failed to start when the network cable was plugged in. I started to believe something that wasn't actually true simply because it made sense to me. Luckily, I also believed I would eventually find the real problem, which I later did. (It was the presence of a specific icon on the Windows XP desktop. Removing it solved the problem permanently.)

## *Tangible Evidence for New Beliefs*

It's always easiest to believe what we're able to see with our own eyes, hear with our own ears, and touch with our own hands. We believe the book in front of us exists because we see it and feel it. We believe someone is calling when we hear the phone ringing. We believe money is desirable because we see so many people working for it.

When we experience something for ourselves, we instantly KNOW it's possible. Our level of belief is 100%. When someone else tells us about an experience, we evaluate the information first before accepting it. How reliable is the source of the information? Has this person lied to us before, or are they trustworthy? Does the information seem plausible? How likely is it to have happened, especially to the person concerned? If we doubt any aspect of the information, its influence on us is reduced proportionately.

For example, even though I don't believe that our planet is being visited by alien spaceships, and the evidence I've seen and heard has been less than ideal, the sheer number of reports has caused me to wonder if there might be something to the story. Each report by a less than perfect eye witness has influenced my beliefs a little bit at a time, and the many reports together have raised my level of belief to the point where I'm now willing to take a closer look.

This happens to everyone. Every time we hear or read another story about someone who has transformed their life by changing a belief, it becomes easier to believe we can also do it. That's why I felt it was important to share my story with you in this book.

This is also why any time one of my coaching clients tells me that what they'd like to do is 'impossible', I suggest they read stories about others who have been in their position and done what they'd like to do. Consider the example of a 50-year-old woman who wanted to start a new career, but felt it was 'impossible' at her age. After reading about a dozen 50+ women who success-fully started new careers, suddenly it wasn't so impossible.

The *"Chicken Soup for the Soul"* series of books has been one of the most successful of the last decade, primarily because they include stories about lots of people doing what we'd like to do ourselves. I fell in love with the Joseph Murphy and Catherine Ponder books for the same reason — they shared many stories of others who have used non-physical means (affirmative prayer) to create desired changes.

## *Creative Daydreaming*

Learning about others who have accomplished what we'd like to do ourselves is a great way to build our belief, but what if we're trying to do something no one has done before? Or what if reading about others isn't enough?

Each and every one of us was born with an incredible gift of imagination. As kids, we played games and pretended to be cops and robbers, cowboys and Indians, kings and queens. For brief periods of time we tried on a new life like many people try on a new outfit before purchasing.

This same imagination we used as children can be used again today to imagine unknown possibilities. Scientists use this same ability to imagine the inside an atom or a black hole. Inventors use this ability to imagine how to put more features into the latest cell phone or alarm clock. Musicians use this ability to create new songs. Business people use this ability to anticipate the next big craze and how they may profit from it.

Psychologists have told us for years that our subconscious mind (the part that keeps track of our many beliefs) cannot tell the difference between an actual experience and one vividly imagined. This means that if we daydream about a desired experience in enough detail, our minds respond as if we had a real experience, and our belief in its possibility grows. In actual practice, few of us can imagine an experience in enough detail to completely fool ourselves, but even with less vivid imagery, it's still a powerful process.

Many people who attempt to daydream creatively remain aware of the furniture they are sitting or laying on, or they imagine the experience somehow differently than they would perceive it in the real world. This reduces the effectiveness of the process.

For many years, I used to imagine things as if they happened in a small space inside my head, or in another dimension of space. It was distinctly different from the world around me, and I felt it. Once I realized the impact of this difference, I adjusted my visualizations to match my perceptions of the real world.

Our inner (subconscious) mind notices the perceptual differences and takes them into consideration when forming beliefs. Thus, you may believe yourself to be confident and a great lover when you're alone, but something completely different when face to face with an attractive stranger.

For maximum impact on our beliefs, we want to convince our inner mind that we are, in fact, face to face with someone in the real world, although we may actually be alone on our couch.

Despite what many 'experts' may claim, the visualization process itself doesn't make anything happen, but is a tool to help build a belief that something COULD happen. It's our beliefs that direct the course of events, not any visualization process. This is why some people can spend many hours 'visualizing' themselves in a desired situation without having it manifest, and why others get everything they want without doing any visualization whatsoever.

As you may recall, I used creative daydreaming as part of my plan to find a wife. During my creative daydreaming sessions, I envisioned many things that had not been a part of any previous relationship, including going to theater, going to fine restaurants, taking vacations around the world, and many other details. The creative daydreaming itself did not produce (or attract) our relationship, yet it did empower me to believe it was possible, which DID produce the desired result. (It's a minor difference, but an important one.) Many of the details I envisioned within the creative daydreaming sessions have been reflected in the relationship I now have with Linda, which indicates the connection between the two.

So how do we use creative daydreaming effectively?

Very easily, and it involves adding one key component to a consciously directed daydream. But before I get too far ahead, let's take a moment, step back, and make sure everyone understands what we're talking about.

Creative daydreaming is a process where we consciously choose to imagine a situation we'd like to experience in the 'real world'. It's like regular daydreaming, but with a purpose — to condition our inner mind to believe the experience we want is not only possible, but already has a history behind it. This creates a strong belief that the same experience will happen again in the future.

For instance, if you'd like to drive a new Jaguar and have never done anything like this before, you can build a belief that it's possible by creatively daydreaming about driving a new Jaguar. If your creative daydream is vivid enough, your inner mind will believe you've done it, and doing it again isn't too far-fetched. This strengthens your belief that it's possible for you to drive a new Jaguar in the future, and helped by the fact that many other people have driven new Jaguars. It is certainly possible!

As another example, if you would like to get a raise at work, imagine getting the raise and everything you'd do with the extra money. Imagine this in as much detail as you can — sights, sounds, feelings, smells, tastes, emotions, everything. Many 'creative visualization' experts recommend doing exactly this.

Now, if we want to take this further, we add another step to the creative daydream. Imagine what led up to the desired experience. For example, what did you *do* to get the raise? Did you get a great idea that saved the company millions of dollars? Did you get an idea that improved a marketing campaign your company is running? Did you introduce your sales manager to a new client who will be worth a lot of money over the coming months? Did you find a cheaper supplier offering higher quality goods?

In addition, imagine the breakthrough event (the reason you got the raise) as a result of something you can consciously choose to do at any time. For instance, imagine that the great new idea came to you as you were watching TV, or while taking a shower, or as you go to work.

When you include 'activation' events into your creative daydream, you instruct your inner mind to produce the desired results in response to regular activities. As you begin to believe this will actually happen, you will soon find yourself paying attention to new things that will eventually lead to you getting that breakthrough idea.

The same process works for any goal you have in mind, even those 'impossible' goals like lifting 3000 pounds, running a mile in five seconds, or being in two places at once. Of course, before such things become possible, you have to believe they can actually happen.

## *Creative Pretending*

We can make creative daydreaming more effective for changing beliefs when we bring the daydream into the real world and act it out. This makes a stronger impression on our inner mind and thus builds a stronger belief. It's also more fun!

Every animal species on this planet has inborn instincts leading them to live healthy and fulfilling lives. Squirrels have an instinct to bury nuts in the Fall in preparation for Winter. Birds have an instinct to build nests in which to lay eggs. Salmon and penguins have an instinct to return to their place of birth to produce the next generation. Humans have an instinct to pretend to be something we would like to become.

As children, we had a natural tendency to pretend. We imitated those people and characters we admired. We imagined what it would be like to live as they lived, testing our own boundaries and limitations to see if we could push past them and become something more than we were.

But somewhere along the way, most of us stopped. We were taught that pretending was just for kids, and that it didn't have any real value in life. Because we trusted those who gave us this information, we accepted their belief and gave up that part of ourselves.

I would like you to give yourself permission to embrace your natural instincts. This may, at first, feel alien to you from the many years of neglect, but will give you more control over your own beliefs. As you do this, you will find yourself enjoying life more and getting the things you truly desire.

There are many different ways we can use the process of pretending to change what we believe. Some people write checks to themselves for $1 million to pretend they are receiving great wealth. Other people carry around a date book filled with names and phone numbers to pretend they are the most popular person around. Many people pretend they are driving a new super sports-car instead of the clunky beater they'd prefer to leave behind. Still others dress up in costume and recite 'magical' poems pretending the words will cause spiritual forces to make changes for them.

All these forms of pretending are good in that they help us believe in something we previously could not. As in all processes designed to create change in the world around us, as long as we believe in the process, it will work for us.

This is true regardless of the process used, including the traditional processes that 'logically' lead to wealth, relationships, health, and so on. Traditional processes such as running a business, investing, dating, charm, prescription drugs, and eating right are only as effective as the beliefs supporting them. We know this because so many people fail even when using such traditional processes.

You can improvise any game of pretend that makes sense in your situation. The more you can 'make it real', the better it will work for you.

If you are a budding author and you'd like to have your next book accepted by a major publisher, type out a letter of acceptance that looks like it came from them and pin it up on your wall. Every time you look at it, think, "I've been accepted once, I can do it again." The next time you submit a manuscript, you'll have a stronger belief in being accepted.

If you have a house for sale, each time you see it, say to yourself, "I used to own that house." and pretend you're on your way somewhere else. On the other hand, if you're looking to buy a home, pretend you already live there and are taking care of it. Just don't trespass onto someone else's property in the process.

If it's a car you'd like to purchase, go to the dealership and take a test drive. As you're in the car, pretend that you have already bought it, and feel the pride of ownership.

On two separate occasions, I used the power of pretending to acquire a vehicle I could not afford otherwise. While driving the car I had at the time, I vividly imagined the sights and sensations of the vehicle I wanted, and in so doing, changed my beliefs about the type of car I owned. In one case, the car I wanted was given to me, and in the other, I was directed to find exactly what I wanted for much less than it was worth.

Whether those 'lucky breaks' occurred because something changed in the outer world, or simply because I became aware of opportunities that existed previously doesn't really matter. What counts is that my experience changed as a result of changing my beliefs.

Many business experts suggest that a person pretend to be successful in order to attract enough customers and clients to become successful. This has been recommended so often, it's now a popular phrase — "fake it 'til you make it." Part of the process works on the beliefs held by other people (they see evidence that suggests you are already successful), and another part of the process affects the beliefs of the individual looking for success. Clearly, the process works for a lot of people. It can work for you as well.

## *Prayer*

Many people understand the process of prayer to be a call for help to a Divine Being capable of providing that help. As with everything else, the process works when you believe in it.

While some will claim they have actually had contact with a Divine Being, psychologists say the experience could simply be a hallucination. That being the case, and despite the long history of Divine interaction with humans, there's no way to prove whether a Divine Being exists or not.

However, it may not matter whether a Divine Being exists or not. If you believe that such a being can answer prayers, then asking for their help is a valid method of tapping into the power of belief even if no Divine Being is there to hear and respond.

Most religions teach that their particular Divine Being will respond to prayers depending on how well the 'sacraments' of the religion are kept. This requires a greater commitment than simply offering a prayer, and involves every aspect of the way you live your life.

In some religions, you have to deny all worldly pleasures in order to be 'pure' and worthy of Divine dispensation, and even then prayers may only be offered for another person. In other religions, the only restriction is that your prayer cannot involve harming another person. In still other religions, anything goes, as long as you are true to yourself.

Some may define prayer as an example of using creative pretending, while others have a firm belief that anything suggesting their particular religion may be false is heresy.

## *Affirmations & Affirmative Prayer*

In the history of belief management, one of the primary tools taught and used has been the simple affirmation. For those who aren't familiar with this term, an affirmation is a statement of what you'd like to experience, stated as though it were already true. An affirmative prayer is a series of affirmations involving a Divine Being. In some respects, using affirmations is pretending on a purely mental level.

In actual fact, everyone uses affirmations whether we realize it or not. Any time we make a statement, we are 'affirming' its truth. In most cases, this is not pretending, but merely expressing a current belief. As mentioned earlier, we can listen to what we say during a day to find out much of what we now believe.

Because what we say generally matches what we believe, our minds grow to associate one with the other. We can use this established relationship in reverse to reshape our beliefs. It's like how you can feel more energized and confident by standing up straight and pulling your shoulders back. Normally, your posture responds to your feelings, but you can change how you feel by changing your posture. Your mind associates feelings and posture so that either one can control the other. The same is true with speech and beliefs. Your mind associates what you say with what you believe.

You've probably heard the joke about the guy who told a lie so often he started to believe it himself. This demonstrates how our minds work. We learn by repetition. When we hear an idea expressed often enough, even one we initially know is false, we eventually reach a point of acceptance and start to wonder if the idea could be true. When the idea is expressed further, we no longer wonder if it might be true because we genuinely believe it to be true.

The common practice of using affirmations starts by creating a statement of the desired results. Many of those who teach this technique will suggest that the affirmation must be stated in present tense and be phrased positively, as in "I will" rather than "I won't." The reasoning for this is based on scientific studies proving that our inner (subconscious) mind interprets everything in present tense and reacts to everything stated, including those things preceded by the word 'not'. (As in "Do NOT think of a pink elephant wearing a lacy tutu.")

While these guidelines do help, they are not absolutely necessary. I have seen many people successfully use affirmations such as "I won't get that job." and "I bet it's going to rain on our picnic tomorrow." Unfortunately, these affirmations are about experiences we'd rather avoid than attract. Either way, the reinforced beliefs produce results just as reliably as any other type of affirmation.

For those readers who have not come across this idea before, here are some examples of how affirmations should be phrased for maximum effectiveness:

- I do well on tests. My mind relaxes and recalls easily the answers to all questions. I am proud of my results.
- Money comes easily to me. I am a fountain of great ideas that produce abundant wealth. I am able to gain the cooperation of others where needed because they enjoy helping me succeed.
- I am a NON-smoker. I breathe clean, fresh air. I am able to calm my nerves simply by setting an intention to do so. Like all non-smokers, I am more attractive than those who put disgusting cigarettes into their mouths.

As you can see, good affirmations state positive beliefs about what is desired, as if it is a current reality. The best affirmations state the desired result as if it happens on it's own without effort or attention. Emotion adds extra power.

Once an affirmation is created, your job is to repeat it often to yourself, out loud if possible. The more you repeat your affirmation, the more you get used to the idea, and the more familiar an idea is, the easier it is to believe. Speaking your affirmation out loud adds the experience of hearing the words, giving the overall experience more dimension and greater substance. Writing the words on paper adds two extra dimensions — sight and physical movement. Each dimension added increases the affirmation's effect on your beliefs.

Measure the strength of your belief before you begin with a question such as "Do I believe that I will _____?" (filling in the blank with your current goal), and then ask the same question again after repeating your affirmation several times. You'll notice the strength of your belief will shift and change.

## *Hammering Iron in a Magnetic Field*

Although using affirmations works wonderfully for many people, there are some who have not seen the results they would like. Most of us in this field have met at least one person who has repeated a good affirmation thousands of times over many months, sometimes years, without any appreciable results.

If you've ever had this experience, you know how frustrating it can be. I had the same problem myself, and if it had not been for a unique discovery, I would have given up and forgotten all about the power of belief.

I wish I could remember where I found this idea so I could give credit where it's due. The idea that turned me around and gave my affirmations new life was the concept of hammering iron in a magnetic field. You see, metal responds to magnetic fields in peculiar ways. Not only is metal attracted to a magnet, but the metal itself can become a magnet in certain circumstances, such as when struck repeatedly while in a magnetic field.

When the metal is struck by a hammer, it's atoms vibrate and realign themselves with the magnetic field. With each blow of the hammer, a few more atoms realign themselves. Eventually, if the metal remains in a fixed relationship to the magnetic field, most of its atoms become aligned in a single direction, causing it to behave as a magnet.

When we use affirmations, it's like we're the metal and the affirmations are the hammer. Each time we repeat an affirmation, it's like the metal is being struck by the hammer and a few atoms of belief are realigned. After enough repetitions, our belief takes on the alignment of the magnetic field surrounding us.

But what is the magnetic field? *It's our feelings!*

Those who see results from using affirmations are those who have a strong feeling of confidence (belief) in the process, whereas those who fail to see results lack confidence in the process. Our level of belief in the process determines the response we see, just as the level of belief in a placebo. If we have a strong belief that it will fail, it will. And just as surely, if we have a strong belief that results will be forthcoming, they will be.

The same has been said about prayer for thousands of years. In order to get results from prayer, you have to believe in the process. With our new grasp of the power belief has in our lives, this is easier to understand.

When we truly understand that it is our belief in a process which produces results, not the process itself, we are free to use any process we choose to create the desired results.

## *Hypnosis*

One process in which millions of people have a strong belief is hypnosis. Although we could interpret this as a game we play with ourselves, it is based on two logical premises — that relaxation reduces the amount of conscious resistance to new ideas, and the use of affirmations to 'program' new beliefs into our inner (subconscious) mind.

This is probably a good time to explain why I tend to use the phrase 'inner mind' rather than 'subconscious mind' as many others do. Traditional psychology (and hypnotism) teaches that the inner mind is below (or outside) our conscious awareness and is thus 'sub-conscious' ('sub', meaning 'below'). However, it's possible to gain awareness within the inner level of mind (such as when someone develops the ability to consciously control their heart rate or blood pressure), and therefore it is not always below the level of consciousness. Because this level of mind is not *necessarily* subconscious, I tend to use the phrase 'inner mind'.

Linguistics aside, there are several techniques that fit under the heading of hypnosis. There's self-directed hypnosis, recorded hypnosis, and operator-directed hypnosis.

Standard self-directed hypnosis (commonly called "self-hypnosis") is a process where you relax (while sitting in a chair or lying down) and repeat affirmations to yourself. As mentioned before, relaxing helps to reduce any conscious resistance to new ideas, helping to eliminate doubts and realign the magnetic field of belief in the process.

Some people relax by first tightening up their muscles and then releasing, helping the muscles relax further with each repetition. Other people relax by suggesting to themselves that each part of their body is now relaxing, as in "My feet are relaxing, my legs are becoming more relaxed, my stomach is relaxing and letting go, my arms are relaxing and becoming limp and loose." Use whatever method you believe will help you relax and enter into a self-hypnotic trance.

Once you feel yourself becoming disassociated from the world around you (a sure sign that you are in the hypnotic trance), the next step is to start repeating one or more affirmations to represent what you'd like to believe. The hard part of this is to remain conscious enough to hold onto your chosen affirmations, and at the same time release conscious control to your inner mind.

Within a single self-hypnosis session, work on only one or two main beliefs. Any more will diffuse your efforts. However, you can include as many supporting beliefs as required to recondition yourself to the major belief. For instance, in one session you can work on your beliefs about relationships, and in another session you can work on your beliefs about money. If you can focus your hypnotic session even further, such as on your beliefs about your motivations for wanting more money, or your expectations of how others will respond to you having more freedom, you'll see quicker results.

When creating affirmations for supporting beliefs, remember the four levels of belief we talked about earlier. Address universal beliefs, world beliefs, self-image beliefs, and surface beliefs. Use the belief archeology process I gave you in Chapter 4 to discover your specific beliefs surrounding the main issue, and create an affirmation for each one needing adjustment. Even better, create two or more for each one, phrasing each affirmation slightly differently. This gives your inner mind more 'fiber' to use in digesting the new material.

I've had lots of people ask me how long a self-hypnosis session should last. What I have found is that there are three main parts of a hypnotic session, the induction (where you relax), the conditioning (where you suggest inner changes), and the resurfacing (where you awaken to the outer world). It takes between 10 and 20 minutes to relax completely, especially when you are guiding yourself through the process. Resurfacing takes less time, usually between one and five minutes. Together, we have between 11 and 25 minutes for these stages. The conditioning portion is the most variable, and you can choose to spend anywhere from one minute to many hours on your mental conditioning.

Before you begin your self-hypnotic session, you may want to set a timer to awaken you. This can be as simple as an oven timer or as complex as a CD alarm clock that awakens you with a series of pre-recorded suggestions. Having a timer allows you to concentrate on the process without being concerned about spending too much time in trance.

Some people prefer to record their affirmations and play the recording after they've relaxed completely. Others prefer to use professionally produced recordings, believing the affirmations will be 'better' and spoken with more authority, and thus easier to believe. Either way, the general guideline is for the affirmations to be spoken slowly, clearly, and with complete confidence that they are conditioning your mind as desired.

Many people prefer to have a professional hypnotist guide them through the process. This has certain advantages over self-hypnosis, as the hypnotist can deliver the affirmations and other suggestions in a calm, confident manner that is quite effective. Most people are able to reach deeper levels of trance. Another advantage is that the professional hypnotist can help discover beliefs you were unable to find yourself and respond to nuances needing to be addressed in the process.

When choosing a professional hypnotist, make sure to ask about their training and background, but more importantly, ask about their beliefs. If you go to a hypnotist who believes life is hard and full of disappointments, those beliefs will likely come across during the conditioning sessions. You want a hypnotist who already believes in the things you're trying to accomplish. Finding a compatible hypnotist is as important as finding a compatible mate.

## *Conversational Hypnosis*

Many people are surprised to learn that you don't have to be in a trance to be hypnotized. Many of the most powerful hypnotic techniques were developed in counseling sessions by trained hypnotherapists. With these techniques, the subject doesn't even know he or she is being hypnotized!

In the 1970's a new science called NLP (Neuro-Linguistic Programming) was born. John Grinder and Richard Bandler worked with several highly competent psycho-therapists to discover the secrets of how the mind works and how to implement changes. Among those studied was a hypnotherapist named Milton Erickson, who had developed unique ways to help his clients. Erickson's contribution to NLP became known as conversational hypnosis.

Over the past few decades, these techniques have been used by professional persuaders in all fields — sales, marketing, politics, religion, and many others. These techniques have even been taught to socially-challenged individuals as a means of attracting and seducing members of the opposite sex.

Although the techniques of conversational hypnosis have been employed as persuasion tactics, we must remember that they originally started out as methods to help therapy clients find better ways of approaching life. (For more information, go to www.KeysToPowerPersuasion.com.)

At the heart of conversational hypnosis is the concept of using the natural tendencies of the mind to facilitate change. It's similar to how a sailor uses the natural tendency of the wind to push the boat across the water. By changing the position of the sails, the boat can go in any direction regardless of the way the wind is blowing. No effort is expended by the boat, but is supplied by the natural tendency of the wind.

Our minds have a natural tendency to associate things together. It's part of the learning process hard-wired into us at the core. For example, if we fall in love while listening to a particular song, we will tend to associate this song with falling in love, and anytime we hear it again, the same feelings will well up within our heart.

If someone knew about our response to this particular song, they could use it to cause us to fall in love with them by making sure the same song played any time we were together. Although our memory may be of someone else, our minds would associate the two people together, making the transference of feelings from one to the other possible.

For our purposes, the main response we want to elicit is the feeling of trust and confidence. Once we learn how to elicit a feeling of confidence unattached to any particular memory, we can then use it to make any belief stronger.

The great thing about conversational hypnosis is that it works quickly. You may have heard about people who can help others eliminate lifelong fears in a matter of minutes. They do it with conversational hypnosis. By using the same techniques to change what you believe, you will see very dramatic results in a matter of minutes.

## *Pacing and Leading Affirmations*

The first conversational hypnosis technique we will explore is the process called "pacing and leading." By 'pacing' a person's current beliefs, we can elicit the feeling of trust and confidence. Once this is done, we can then 'lead' that person to believe new things. Here's a brief example of how this is usually done in a hypnosis session:

> "As you sit there on the couch, listening to my words, with the sounds of traffic coming in through the window, and taking a moment to notice the inflow and the outflow of your breathing, you are beginning to relax."

With the above example, the hypnotist is pacing the patient's current beliefs by mentioning things that are obvious and identifiable. The patient is sitting. On the couch. Listening to the hypnotist's words. Hearing the sounds of traffic coming in from the window. Noticing the inflow and outflow of his/her breathing. Five things that are absolutely true. This elicits within the patient a feeling of "yes, the hypnotist is telling the truth — I can trust what is being said."

Immediately after this feeling is elicited, the hypnotist leads the patient to a new belief — "you are beginning to relax." The feeling of trust brought forth with the pacing statements is automatically associated with this new statement, and the patient now believes they are beginning to relax. This belief is immediately reflected in the patient's experience. He or she relaxes.

Other aspects are involved in this sort of hypnotic induction. As the hypnotist mentions the patient's breathing, the patient automatically turns his or her attention to it. This has two effects. First, this allows the patient to accept the hypnotist's suggestion that they are taking a moment to notice their breathing, and thus sets up an additional pacing statement. And second, this directs the patient to turn his or her attention within, which has a natural tendency to cause one to relax.

Between all of these conversational hypnotic effects, the patient has an experience of 'responding' to the hypnotist's suggestions, which leads to a more successful therapy session.

We can use this same technique on ourselves to help change what we believe. All we have to do is elicit a feeling of trust and belief by 'affirming' what is obviously true, and then lead ourselves into a new belief.

One way of thinking about this is to realize that the pacing statements are eliciting emotions which act as the magnetic field in which you are hammering the iron of your beliefs. The stronger the magnetic field (your emotions), the quicker your beliefs will change.

Another good way of thinking about this process is to imagine a field of energy (trust and confidence) being created with the pacing statements. Once your field of energy is strong and vital, the leading statement is placed within that energy field and conditioned by it. Thus, the feelings of trust and confidence are transferred to the objective belief.

For example, let's say that we want to experience a greater degree of financial abundance in our lives. After exploring our current beliefs, we find that the main belief standing in our way is something like "I'll never make any real money working for my current employer. They are only out for themselves and will squeeze as much as they can from me."

Most companies today do seem to be focused on the 'bottom line' and how much profit they can generate. However, what most of us tend to miss is that most companies reward employees who help them earn more profits. If you were to present a plan to save your company millions over the next couple of years, or increase sales by 30%, they are sure to reward you with a raise, or a bonus, or maybe even both.

So after due consideration, you've decided to choose to believe that you can make a lot of money working for your current employer. You may not yet have that winning idea, but in order to facilitate it's arrival, you want to clear the pathway with a more empowering belief.

In order to use the concept of pacing and leading affirmations, start out by choosing a set of pacing affirmations. To do this, simply note down a few things that are absolutely true, especially things that relate to your desired objective.

Here is an example set of pacing and leading affirmations:

1. I work for ABC Corporation.
2. We are in the business of selling widgets.
3. I am responsible for shipping widgets.
4. I like many of my co-workers.
5. I would like to earn more money.
6. I can find a way to help ABC save money on shipping widgets.
7. ABC will reward me for my insightful plan.

In the above affirmations, the first five are purely pacing affirmations, statements that are absolutely true and are already believed 100%. The last two affirmations focus on beliefs you may want to strengthen. Affirmation number six is easy to believe and supports the final affirmation, the main objective here.

You may want to measure the strength of your belief in the final statement before you start, and then again afterwards, to see how well the process works. This will help your future efforts be more effective.

So, before you get started, ask yourself, "How much do I believe that ABC will reward me for helping them save money?" Imagine your gauge and see where that belief registers. If you have to, calibrate the gauge first with questions that produce both "absolute YES" or "absolute NO" answers, such as "Do I believe I know my own name?" or "Do I believe I am a squirrel?"

Now repeat your list of affirmations a few times. Five to ten times is enough to start. Measure the strength of your belief in that last leading statement again. Notice how much stronger it is now than it was just a minute or two before. Now you have proof of how well this process works.  Go ahead and repeat the list of affirmations a few more times.

There is no rule about how many times you should repeat the same list of affirmations.   My suggestion is to measure the strength of the objective belief from time to time and stop when you feel it's strong enough.  This may happen after 5 repetitions of the list, or after 20.  Every situation is unique.

For some situations, you may find that the objective belief doesn't seem to be growing at all.   When this happens, it's because there are other beliefs that need to be worked on first.  If you notice this, go back to Chapter 4, find the responsible beliefs, and work on the more general beliefs first.  As a guide, work on Universal Beliefs first, World Beliefs second, Self-Image Beliefs next, and Surface Beliefs last.

Some people feel they need to change the list of pacing affirmations from time to time.  If you believe this, then you'll need to adjust them periodically.  Maybe you'd prefer to choose to believe that a single set of pacing affirmations can work every time.  Or maybe you'd prefer to use a shortcut and bypass the pacing affirmations completely.


## *Faith Anchoring*

Pacing affirmations can be a quick and easy tool for eliciting feelings of trust and confidence.  Yet, it's possible to bypass them completely and get results that are just as good.

Once again, the concept of "anchoring" comes from conversational hypnosis and uses the natural tendency of the mind to associate things together.  An "anchor" is anything that triggers the arousal of a feeling or thought.  The song that reminds you of falling in love is an anchor.  A smile that makes you feel welcome and accepted is an anchor.  A loud noise that frightens you is an anchor.  A tone of voice can be an anchor if it elicits a particular feeling, as can the way someone walks or sits across a piece of furniture. Words themselves can also be anchors if they elicit strong emotion.

Those who use conversational hypnosis are able to create specific anchors in a matter of minutes, and then proceed to use them to control feelings within the clients they work with. These anchors range from normal things like tone of voice and gestures, to a particular way of touching a person's arm, or even which eye they are looking at when speaking particular phrases.

Under the control of a master conversational hypnotist, anchors can be used to subtly direct a person to feel or believe just about anything. A demonstration of this on the TV show "*Mind Control with Derren Brown*" proved that a person can be reprogrammed to believe that yellow is red and red is black, all within what appears to be an innocent conversation.

While this may be used to 'brainwash' and manipulate someone, we can use the same techniques for positive change, which is why the process was originally developed.

There are two ways of working with anchors. You can either use pre-existing anchors or create new ones. Pre-existing anchors are the easiest to use because you don't have to spend any time creating them. Creating new anchors takes more time, but can actually be better because you have complete control over them.

Take a moment to think about how you can identify if someone is telling the truth, or how you can tell if someone is confident in themselves. The things you list are your anchors for truth and confidence.

For most of us, when we see someone standing tall, with shoulders back and chest thrust forward, and speaking with a firm, clear voice, we assume that he or she is confident. For confidence, our anchors are posture and voice tone.

To carry this further, if we recall a time when we felt highly confident and let this feeling take over our bodies, we will find that our backs become straighter and we breathe deeper. This is our natural association with confidence.

We can use this natural association to elicit a feeling of confidence when we want to strengthen a belief. To be more specific, all we have to do is consciously activate the anchor (by straightening our backs and breathing deeper, for instance) and then think about our objective belief.

Like the process of using pacing and leading affirmations, activating an anchor can be thought of as creating a field of energy into which the objective thought is placed. This has the effect of transferring the feeling elicited by the anchor to the thought expressed at that time.

As an example, let's say that you are in the process of negotiating a contract and the other party has just made a comment that causes you to worry about the possible outcome. Because you don't want to repeat a series of pacing and leading affirmations out loud, you consciously choose to take a deep breath and sit up straight. As a feeling of confidence is elicited, you think about your desired outcome, which is a contract written in your favor. Mentally, you picture the outcome and say to yourself, "I'm going to get what I want in this."

As your belief in a successful negotiation is strengthened, it is reflected in your experience and the rest of the negotiation process moves towards the desired outcome. It may seem like magic, but it's the natural flow of the universe, as we saw in Chapter 1.

Posture and deep breathing are not the only anchors you'll find within yourself, although they are perhaps the easiest to identify and describe. I know that, within myself, I associate a certain feeling in my gut with confidence. It's like everything locks in place, and the rest of my being stands on a firmer foundation.

When you spend some time thinking about the nature of confidence within yourself, you will notice your own anchors for this concept. And obviously, you can use the same process to discover your internal anchors for other feelings as well.

Anchors can also be things like how you hold a pen or a cup. Gestures can be anchors. If you have a tendency to bring your hands behind your head when contemplating something you fully expect to enjoy, you can use that gesture to elicit the feeling of joyful expectation, which in turn, can be used to condition new beliefs.

You can create your own anchors fairly easily. The first step is to decide what to use as an anchor. For best results, this should be something that appears natural (for public use), yet is rarely, if ever, found in your normal repertoire of expression.

For example, many people will cross the first two fingers of either hand, yet most will make this expression with their primary hand only. (i.e.- right handed individuals normally cross the fingers of their right hand.) If you're right handed, you can create an anchor where you cross the fingers of your left hand. Or maybe you want to create an anchor where you cross your index finger with your thumb.

Another example is a word said in a particular tone of voice. Although most of us are accustomed to saying the word "yes" from time to time, we rarely say it with excitement and enthusiasm. Also rare is saying the word "yes" and extending the *s*, as in "yesssssssss." Either of these could be used as anchors.

The next step is to elicit the feeling you want to associate with the anchor. The best way to do this is to imagine a time when you felt that emotion very strongly. If you're creating a confidence anchor, remember a time when you felt extremely confident. If you're creating an anchor to elicit the feeling of joy, then remember a time when you were overflowing with joy.

When you feel the emotion as intensely as you possibly can, form the anchor. This means to cross your fingers, say your chosen word with the special emphasis, or whatever you chose for an anchor.

Now remove your anchor (stop doing it) and let the emotion fade away. Repeat the whole process several times; eliciting the desired emotion, applying your anchor when it's at its peak, and then letting it all fade away again. The more you do this, the stronger the association between your new anchor and the elicited emotion will become. If you've done it right, the next time you want to elicit the feeling, all you have to do is to apply your anchor.

Now that you've created a new anchor, the process of using it is the same as with pre-existing anchors. Simply apply your confidence anchor when you think of a belief you want to strengthen, and the natural association process of your mind will make it happen.

## *Using Contrast*

Creating anchors uses a conversational hypnosis principle that we can use separately — the principle of contrast.

The principle of contrast says that different things appear to be *even more* different when next to each other. A good band sounds even better when they follow a poor opening act. A young person seems even younger when sitting next to an older person. Warm water seems almost hot when you're cold. And a kind person appears to be a Saint after you've just been harassed.

Let's say you want to create a new belief that you can easily stand up in front of people and give a talk, but the idea scares you to death. Imagine going to the extreme and being naked in front of a large crowd of people, trying to sing or juggle (assuming that you can't do either). After imagining an extreme situation, the thought of giving a public speech seems much more acceptable, and easier to believe you can do it.

If you want to believe in your ability to go confidently into the boss's office with a great new proposal, but you find the thought frightening, think about trying to order the president around, with news cameras and the nation watching. The idea of making a presentation to your boss in the privacy of his office now seems a lot safer, doesn't it?

Or maybe you want to believe you will be healed of a major illness, but feel it's impossible. Spend some time thinking about the multiple-personality patients who create and heal diabetes and other major health issues in seconds as they switch from personality to personality. Or think about the cases where conditions like cancer have healed within days in response to placebos.  Now the idea that your condition will heal quickly seems much more likely.

## *Associative Linking*

Conversational hypnosis is a powerful tool for changing beliefs because the way we present an idea carries more meaning than the actual words themselves.

Consider the phrase, "as sure as the sun will rise tomorrow." On the surface, we all know this means that whatever the speaker is referring to can be counted on.  However an additional meaning is also assumed.  We assume the fact that the sun will rise tomorrow can be counted on as well.

We hear examples of this in normal, everyday conversation, and over time our minds have associated the syntax of the phrase (the grammatical structure) with the fact that whatever comes after "as sure as" is generally an incontestable reference point.

We can use this association to suggest that some idea can be trusted and considered a fact, by using it in a phase like "as sure as I'm getting a raise next week."  This suggests the referenced raise is something we can count on.

The phrase "as sure as" is not the only phrase of this type.  A full range of words can be used in place of "sure."  Other examples include "as quick as," "as easy as," "as rich as," and "as healthy as."

It's also possible to suggest a link between two ideas simply by expressing them one after the other, as in "The sun shone brightly on the baseball diamond.  The kids played badly." Although the speaker doesn't explicitly say so, it is suggested that the sun CAUSED the kids to play badly.

Whenever two ideas are expressed together, our minds have a natural tendency to assume a link between them.  We can use this to create or strengthen our beliefs.  Here are some examples of this:

- The number of wireless communication devices has doubled in recent years. I need to buy a cell phone.
- There are over 6.5 billion people in the world. There are a lot of people interested in what I have to say.
- There are more millionaires now than there ever has been before. It's easy to make money now.
- I am reading this book. My life is getting better.
- My life has been hard. God has a special plan for me.
- I have blond hair. People go out of their way for me.
- I think intently about the things I want. They are being attracted into my life.
- The sky is blue. I'm going to be famous.

The point to notice in these examples is that there really isn't any special connection between the first statement and the second. As the author of this book, I'd *like* to believe your life will improve simply because you're reading it, however, your life will improve only if you USE the information I'm giving you.

Regardless of whether or not any connection exists between one statement and the next, you can use this format to create beliefs which support and empower you in achieving your goals and dreams. Believing you will be famous just because the sky is blue is as valid a reason as any other. There really doesn't HAVE to be a logical reason to believe anything. Your belief will be reflected in your life experience regardless.

We can have a lot of fun with this. We can choose to believe that *anything* can be the reason for our success and happiness, including those things we previously believed were obstacles and limitations.


## *Submodality Modification*

If you were to imagine the feeling of confidence as a color, what color would it be? If it were a sound, would the pitch be high or low? And if you could touch it with your hands, would it be smooth or textured? Your answers to these questions reveal some of the inner associations your mind has to the feeling of confidence.

Experts say that each of us has a preferred 'modality' of thinking. Some of us are visual thinkers, and have a tendency to 'see' thoughts, ideas, and feelings. Others are auditory and think of things in terms of sounds. And another group are called kinesthetics because they relate to the world around them in terms of physical sensation. A very tiny minority of folks focus on other modalities, such as gustatory and olfactory — relating to the world by taste and smell respectively.

Although we use other modalities from time to time, we generally tend to focus on one more often than the others. This is another technique used in conversational hypnosis to help people communicate more effectively. When you speak to someone "in their language," they respond more readily to your requests.

So if you know that someone is a visual-centric person, use phrases such as "I see what you mean" or "That's a very bright idea." If you're dealing with an auditory-centric person, use phrases such as "That sounds good to me" or "There's a ring of truth about this." And for a kinesthetic person, use phrases like "This feels good" or "Do you grasp what I'm saying?"

It's fairly easy to discover someone's preferred modality. Simply listen to them and notice which type of phrases they use most often. In fact, you can do this with yourself to find your own preferred modality if you're not quite sure. Once you know this, you can use it to enhance your belief-work.

Here's a very brief and simple overview of how this works. If you discover that your mind tends to record positive expectations in blue ink and negative expectations in red ink, you can change a negative expectation simply by imagining it in blue ink. This is a simple example of manipulating a visual modality of thinking using the submodality of color.

When you think of the characteristics involved in a visual image, you realize that color, brightness, clarity, apparent distance (how close or far away the image is), location (in front, back, left, right, up, down, etc.), and size are all involved. If the image is moving, speed is also involved.

Auditory submodalities include pitch, tone, loudness, rhythm, harmony, clarity (clear or muffled), and location.

Submodalities related to the kinesthetic modality include size, weight, texture, density (soft or hard), pressure, temperature, shape, and location.

We use this information to alter our beliefs by first noticing how our minds have recorded a concept we believe 100%. Think of something you are absolutely sure of, and write down a description of it. If it's a visual image, what colors are involved? How big is the image? How bright is it? Where is the image placed in your mind? Is it front and center, or is it placed to the left or right, up or down, near or far? If it's more auditory, where is the sound coming from? What pitch seems to be more dominant? Describe the thought in as many details as possible.

To take this further, describe your mental recording of several things that you believe in 100%. This will reveal common threads running through them. These common threads indicate how your mind records a firm belief. Once you know how your mind records a firm belief, you can add the same characteristics to any belief you want to strengthen.

As an example, let's say you've found your firm beliefs to generally be associated with bright, clear images, more or less front and center in your mind. Let's also say you want to believe that relationships can be easy and you will find someone with whom you will experience great joy and satisfaction.

If you notice that when you think about the possibility of having such a relationship, the image is dull, dark, and seems to be at a great distance away, you can change the belief simply by bringing the image closer, making it brighter, and bringing it into clear sharp focus. In effect, you are rewriting the thought in blue ink instead of red ink.

You may need to do this several times before the belief is completely rewritten in your mind. When this happens, your mind will automatically bring up the new image with all the characteristics representing trustworthiness, and your expectation of a positive outcome will be strong.

And because your expectation is strong, your belief in finding a joyous and satisfying relationship will be reflected in the world around you — you will actually be in that relationship quicker than you can now imagine.

On the surface level, it doesn't seem logical that simple changes in mental images can have such dramatic effects in the world around us, but the fact is that it works. Millions of people all over the world have seen results from these techniques, sometimes in ways that are miraculous and even 'spooky'.

## *Belief Leverage*

Now we move away from conversational hypnosis techniques and move into a subject with a much longer history. For some, this section will seem to be purely superstition, and for others, this will seem to be magic. However you now think of it, we're going to have a lot of fun.

To fully understand the power of belief leveraging, we have to recall the power of placebos to heal. When a patient is given a sugar pill, there is nothing in the pill to heal the patient's condition, yet they are healed because they *believe* they will be.

According to many doctors, the results many people obtain when wearing copper or magnetic bracelets are also evidence of the placebo effect, as are the results from 'energy therapies' like Reiki.

These techniques work when the patient believes in them. The placebo effect is based on leveraging a patient's belief to effect a healing. It all comes back to the common phrase "it only works if you believe in it," which we have turned around to say "if you believe in it, it will work."

Literally anything can be used to release the power of the placebo effect. Lighting a candle to create an atmosphere of financial abundance is one method used by many. Wearing crystals to 'charge' the aura and ease communications is another. Sitting inside a large pyramid shape to heighten spirituality is yet another example. Saying a prayer is also an example. Performing ceremonial magick with robes, candles, incense, magic symbols, and speaking 'spells', is a more involved form of using the placebo effect.

Although there is no logical reason for any of these to produce any kind of result, they do when those using them believe in the process. The belief one has in the process is leveraged to increase a belief in the objective.

It's relatively easy to understand how a belief in healing may have a result. After all, our minds *do* handle the healing process of our bodies and there is a direct connection between the two. It's less clear how a belief within our own mind can change what another person may feel or choose to do. It's also less obvious how a belief in prosperity can bring additional opportunities and more money into our lives.

Whether or not we *understand* how something works does not change the fact that it *does* work. Few of us understand how our minds can remember a fact, yet it happens quite often. Few of us understand how electricity actually works, yet we are happy to use it frequently for many tasks. Just because we don't fully understand how a change in belief can produce changes in the world around us is no reason to deny ourselves the opportunity to use this principle.

When we allow ourselves to have fun with the process, we can once again be like children and play our favorite games, knowing that, by playing, we are being productive in new and exciting ways.

Of course, the underlying principle here is that you must believe in whatever process you choose to use. If you believe you can dress up in robes and wave a magic wand around to attract more money into your life, then by all means do so. If you believe you can imagine a pyramid around you and have that image open your psychic senses, then go for it!

On the other hand, if you believe that you have to study, work hard, and persevere in order to succeed, then you'll fail until you take those steps.  At least, until you choose a new set of beliefs about what is required for success.

In a similar way, if you believe that only God (or pharmaceuticals) can heal, then you must abide by that belief unless, and until, you choose to change that belief to a more empowering belief in yourself.

In the next chapter, we'll take a look at how we can use belief leverage to make changing beliefs easier.

## *Keys To Power Principles*

Belief Leverage forms the foundation for my *Keys To Power* system.  Within this system, a practitioner believes the following:

1. God created the Universe and all things therein.
2. All created things (including us) are composed of the essence of God.
3. Because this essence of God is all-powerful, and may be called anything, we choose to simply call it Power.
4. By aligning ourselves with the nature of God, we become open to the flow of Power.  God does not decide who may use this Power; it is available to all.
5. As Power flows through us, it picks up our thoughts, feelings, and beliefs, and uses these to create our reality.
6. We have been given the capability and responsibility to create our lives as we wish.  We do this through the thoughts and feelings we focus upon.
7. We may improve our ability to direct Power to create desired experiences by improving our mental focus and emotional control.
8. There are no limits as to what Power may do.
9. There is no duality of good and evil.  The only duality is of desirable and undesirable.  Undesirable appearances result

from mistaken uses of Power.  A more intelligent use of Power may correct the situation.

10. Living with Love makes Life Wonderful!

As mentioned earlier, I used the *Keys To Power* system to create many personal successes, and it worked because I believed it would.  The central concepts revolve around an energy, thought to come from a Divine Being, flowing through our minds and emotions on its way towards creating our reality.

A similar set of principles form the foundation in *"Harmonic Prayer."*  In the Harmonic Prayer system, the core belief is that prayer works best when three factors are in place — faith, focus, and a feeling of harmony with God.  *"Harmonic Prayer"* draws support from several references to the Christian Bible to help those who have strong religious beliefs.

The same three factors form the foundation in *"Awaken the Avatar Within,"* where they are called confidence, clarity, and connection.  *"Awaken the Avatar Within"* presents the information in a non-religious context, unlike *"Harmonic Prayer."*

All of these books/systems may be found at the PowerKeys Publishing website.  (www.PowerKeysPub.com)

# Chapter 6: Living in a New Reality

We have covered a wide variety of techniques that may be used to change what we believe. You now know *what* to do, although you may be wondering *how* to do it.

When you worked with the material in Chapter 4, you learned how to discover the many different beliefs you have within you. As you found, you have thousands of beliefs about all sorts of things, many of them inter-related to various concepts and goals you may want to accomplish. You may have found a handful of beliefs you want to change, or you may have found hundreds.

## *Work from General to Specific*

When you have a lot of beliefs to change, you'll get the best results when you work from general to specific.

Start with Universal Beliefs first, then work on World-Level Beliefs, followed by Self-Image Beliefs, and finally Surface-Level Beliefs. It's like when building a house, it's best to start with the foundation, then the floor, then the walls, and finally the roof.

Universal Beliefs do not depend on Self-Image Beliefs, and may even reverse the effect of Self-Image Beliefs. In the same way, Surface-Level Beliefs depend on all other levels for support. Going back to the house example, you *could* start by building the roof, but what will support it while you're building the walls? You may end up doing the roof all over again, so you might as well wait until there's something to support it.

Anyone who has failed when working with beliefs has usually made this mistake. They tried to change their Surface-Level beliefs without addressing one or more supporting beliefs. In effect, they tried to build a roof without having four new walls to support it.

When you start with the foundation and build up from there, you will get better results and have an easier time overall.

## *Use the Leverage Principle*

> *Give me six hours to chop down a tree, and I will*
> *spend the first four sharpening the axe.*
> — *Abraham Lincoln, (1809—1865)*
> *16th American President, 1861—1865*

While it's certainly possible to simply dive in and start working on your beliefs about various issues, you'll find that you can accomplish a lot more when you take advantage of the leverage principle.

The idea is to create a set of tools to help you create and change your beliefs. With a specialized set of tools, you can create and change beliefs within minutes or even seconds. Although it takes some time to create these tools, the benefits are worth more than the investment.

Here's an example to demonstrate what I mean. Let's say that you spend five hours working on your beliefs about your job and prosperity in general. The following week, you could spend another three hours working on your beliefs about improving your relationships with your co-workers. And the week after, another seven hours on something else. After three weeks, you've spent fifteen hours doing belief work. Over the course of the next year, you could spend many hours making adjustments to all areas of your life.

Instead of doing all that, if you create a set of 'master beliefs', which act as tools in your belief work, you could accomplish each of the other tasks in MUCH less time.

I can attest to the fact that it's possible to change a belief simply by deciding to do so. Once you have a high level of belief in your ability to change a belief with a simple, conscious choice, the rest of the process is extremely quick and easy.

## *Create a Set of Master Beliefs*

Choosing to believe that it's easy to change beliefs is the first of a set of "master beliefs" you'll want to create.

It's possible to create a belief solely to create or change other beliefs. This is similar to a computer programmer who will create a new piece of software just to make his or her job easier. It's also like a construction crew building a temporary structure to aid in the building of a skyscraper or a bridge.

The principle here is that you create one 'master' belief to make the process of changing or creating other beliefs easier. This 'master' belief can be literally anything, just like a faith anchor, because in essence, that's exactly what it is.

You can create a belief that any time you cross the fingers of your non-dominant hand (left hand for right-handed folks), whatever you focus on will instantly become a 100% level belief. Or you could create a belief that any time you put on a specific piece of jewelry, you automatically believe anything you hear. This can be very useful when you use hypnotic recordings.

This 'master' belief can be created using any of the techniques we discussed in the previous chapter. You can use traditional hypnosis, creative daydreaming, creative pretending, pacing and leading affirmations, or whatever feel right for you.

Once you have created such a tool, you can then use it to establish any belief you desire. If you want to believe in unlimited financial prosperity, you can use your master belief-tool to quickly program your inner mind to expect an abundant flow of money into your life. If you want to attract a more harmonious romantic relationship, you can use this master tool for that as well.

The magical training given to initiates of ancient secret schools of occult traditions used this idea heavily. Mainstream religions use this principle when they 'teach' about the way God responds to prayers. And commercial advertisers use it when promoting their products. The more they convince you that you can get quick and easy results from taking pills, or applying skin creams, or following a prepared plan of action, the more you expect positive results when using those products.

Now that you understand the power of belief itself, you are free to choose whether to accept these teachings or not. Maybe you'd prefer to believe in success and happiness without the aid of commercial products, but then again, maybe you like the idea of using a physical product to look younger, or feel vibrantly healthy, or sleep more soundly.

It's your choice.

In the ancient past, a wide variety of tools were accepted and used on a regular basis to aid in the alteration and formation of beliefs. Amulets, talismans, and magic potions were created and sold as instruments to change beliefs, although they were not described as such. Eventually, science labeled these tools as superstitious nonsense and the world lost faith in them.

In hindsight, we can see that science failed to see the usefulness of such tools because scientists started to believe that everything could be explained in physical terms. Because they believed this, they found evidence supporting their belief, and the circle went 'round and 'round as scientists convinced the rest of the world to believe as they did. Few people want to be seen as "behind the times."

Now that the power of belief is being rediscovered, we realize much of today's modern economy is based on selling products to help us believe in the things we want to experience, such as good health, attracting enjoyable relationships, and living in luxury.

The situation is not so different from the 'old' economy of selling amulets, talismans, and potions to accomplish many of the same things. The forms of products are different, yet the usefulness and expected results are very much the same.

## Focus on Success and Happiness

Sometimes, the easiest way to change your beliefs to the point where you expect success and happiness is to simply choose to interpret every event as being instrumental in helping you experience what you want. Because of the sheer power of such a belief to affect all areas of life, it falls into the 'master belief' category.

My friend, Al Diaz, has taken this concept and formed a system around it. He calls it *"The Titus Concept"* and has already written a couple of books about the idea. Many people have reported amazing transformations in their lives when they've applied even this one simple concept, which, at it's essence, is merely to affirm that everything is, as he says, "for my best and highest good."

When you're looking for a reason why something is for your benefit, you tend to notice things you hadn't noticed when you were thinking that an event or a bit of news could only lead to frustration or problems. As Zig Ziglar has been known to say, "First decide that whatever happens is terrific, then look for a reason why it is so.," or as many motivational speakers say, "When life hands you a lemon, find a way to turn it into lemonade." It can be done far more often than most people realize.

## See Alternate Perspectives

Some of the most powerful beliefs are those defining what something 'means'. For instance, if you're on stage giving a presentation, and you trip over the mic stand and spill a bunch of papers, you have a choice as to whether you define it as a bad experience or something that can bring levity and humor to the presentation. After all, many people enjoy a good comedy more than a formal presentation.

You *could* choose to believe that your audience will listen more intently to your presentation and you now have an opportunity to make a stronger impact.

I've noticed that many people have been taught to interpret negative experiences as if they were God's way of testing us, or helping us learn how to be better people. This can be a beneficial way of looking at things, especially since it allows us to believe there is a purpose and design to unpleasant experiences.

Personally, I believe that when things don't work out, it means I still have more to learn about creating the experiences I want to enjoy. This perspective has led me to discover the principles described in this book, which have empowered me to create the exact lifestyle I desire.

Another way of looking at unhappy experiences is to imagine they are manifestations of previous beliefs and as you work to develop more empowering beliefs, your experiences will change to reflect the new beliefs instead.

One of the worst perspectives to consider is that bad things "just happen" or "that's the way things are." These beliefs prevent us from developing the ability to change events in our lives to more enjoyable ones.

On the other side, one of the best perspectives is to consider that all events and experiences will eventually lead to the realization of one or more of your desired goals.

It's possible to alter our belief systems so that what used to upset us or lead us to expect a negative outcome will trigger a more positive expectation instead. For instance, it's possible to respond to criticism with joy, especially when you believe it can help you improve your results.

A belief held by many is that the universe (or God) is trying to create a better life for you than you could ever imagine, and that the only thing you have to do to live that life is to let go and let it happen. Guy Finley describes this idea quite effectively in his book, *"The Secret of Letting Go."*

This last idea is an excellent 'master belief'.

## *Believe in Magic*

The more you work with your beliefs, and the more you see results that defy explanation, the more you believe in magic.

A common thread running through these 'master beliefs' is the idea that life can be easy, and you don't have to do much work to produce the results you want, because the universe WANTS you to be happy.

Another way of looking at this is to imagine the universe as a magical place where powers greater than gravity, chemistry, or physics are at your command, ready to respond the moment you decide what you want. The only reason you haven't noticed these powers is because they respond according to your belief in them.

If you don't believe in them, they don't respond.

It's very easy to be caught up in the common belief of the universe as a purely physical system of independent entities completely separate from each other. Hopefully, the new scientific discoveries will help to dispel this myth and reveal the power of belief as the true cause behind the events in our lives.

Once you experience the magical power of belief yourself, you'll KNOW, beyond any shadow of a doubt, that the world around you is a direct reflection of your inner beliefs. And once you have this knowing deep within you, you'll never again be fooled by the illusion presented by the physical world.

It isn't necessary to believe in magic genies, fairies, or nature sprites. However, if you *did* believe in them, your belief would create experiences to confirm their existence. Alternately, you could choose to believe in a 'magical' force of nature, such as the Zero-Point Field, or PK (psychokinesis, or 'mind over matter').

Once again, it's another 'master belief' we can create for our personal empowerment. We can choose to believe that we are magical beings living in a magical world, and have simply chosen not to use our incredible power until this moment in time.

## *Manage Your Beliefs*

Many beliefs are formed through our own thought processes. We notice something in our environment, and rather than waiting until we have enough information to really know what it means, we make a random guess at what it means, taking the first step in creating a new belief.

For instance, a driver on the road seems to be driving erratically and cuts us off. We really don't have enough information to know why this happened, however, many of us will prejudge the situation and conclude the driver is a jerk.

For all we know, they could be rushing to someone's aid who has just been hurt in an accident, or trying to escape a coming meteor about to hit the road. Perhaps it might be better to reserve judgment until we have all the facts.

Another example I've noticed with a lot of people is that they have a series of frustrating experiences and start to wonder what might be causing them. Some will say things like "The Universe is against me this week" or "I'm unlucky" or even "God is punishing me."

The problem with these snap judgments is that they form the seed of a belief which eventually colors our whole world. When you think about the possible consequences of a belief that God is against you (a Universal Belief), you'll realize that whatever it is, it's not going to be pleasant. And what about the consequences of believing there is a God who would even consider punishing someone? One belief leads to other related beliefs.

A belief that you are unlucky (a Self-Image Belief) will interfere with any goal you may want to achieve. Even a belief that a specific erratic driver is a jerk (a Surface-Level Belief) can predispose us to believe that people in general can be jerks, which would lead to a host of related experiences.

## *Cultivate Positive Beliefs*

One way to protect yourself from unwanted negative beliefs is to refrain from making uninformed judgments. This takes practice, especially if you've been in the habit for a long time. It's completely unnecessary, however, because what may be the best solution is to continue to 'jump to conclusions', but jump to positive conclusions instead.

This may also take work before it becomes habitual. To automatically assume that everything happens for your benefit, especially when it resembles a negative situation from your past, can seem like Pollyanna thinking. As intelligent beings, we don't want to just stick our heads in the sand like an ostrich and pretend everything is okay when it isn't.

But on the other hand, there are many situations that at first appear to be a disaster with terrible repercussions, yet turn out quite wonderful once we allow ourselves to move through them. When we instantly react as though the experience is bad, we lose the opportunity to experience the hidden joy within.

The bottom line (again) is that the world around us tends to reflect the nature of our beliefs, and when we choose to believe life is wonderful, then we have an easier time achieving the goals we set for ourselves, and experience what some may call 'good luck'.

## *Prepare for the Possibility of Failure*

I'm certainly not advocating the adoption of irresponsible behavior. It's always a smart idea to protect yourself from the possibility of failure, especially during the early phases when you're still practicing your skills in this area. However, it's possible to do so while believing "Plan B" will never be used.

The way to do this is to look at the situation as 99% guaranteed to succeed, with only a 1% chance of failure. When you do this, you can approach the creation of "Plan B" as a safety net 'just in case'. This is one case where it's perfectly acceptable to do something expecting it will be a waste of time.

This helps you feel more prepared and less anxious about the outcome. When you KNOW you're prepared, NO MATTER WHAT, your expectation of ultimate success grows. In the end, it helps propel you forward toward success and a happy ending.

## Build Momentum

You will get excellent results when you start small and build from there. Don't start by trying to believe the 'impossible', like being able to fly, or to lift a car. The easiest way to start is with something you believe is possible.

For example, start by building a belief that you can approach one new person a week and start a conversation if this has been difficult for you. Or start with a belief that you can be more in control of your own life if you've felt out of control before. Or you can start building a belief that you can learn to take more time to relax and be good to yourself.

When you see results, even though they may be small, it becomes easier to believe you can be successful. This helps make the next belief easier to change or develop. And once you've accumulated a series of results, and feel the pride of accomplishment, you'll know you're ready to make more dramatic changes. By building in this way, there's no limit to what you can achieve. As they say, a journey of 1000 miles begins with a single step.

You can help put your goals into perspective by using the principle of contrast and comparing them to 'impossible' goals, like materializing objects out of thin air or teleporting from place to place. Compared to those, becoming healthier, bringing more money into your life, or improving your relationships seem to be rather trivial goals, don't they?

Here's a good example of the effect of taking small steps toward a goal. When I was in high school, I was involved with weight-lifting.  After several years of training, I could bench-press a maximum of 150 pounds.  Many of our school's football players were able to press 220 pounds.  As hard as I tried to push myself, I never seemed to be able to get past the 150 pound level.

I had read the myth of Milo, who lifted a baby calf once a day until it had grown into a full-sized bull.  Each day, the small calf grew by a very small amount, so each lift was only a small step forward for Milo,  Yet when the calf had grown to a full sized bull, Milo was the only one capable of lifting it.  I wanted to try the same thing with my bench-pressing.

So I started with something I KNEW I could do, which was 130 pounds.  That was easy enough.  The next day, I added 2½ pounds to the stack and lifted that.  Once again, a very easy lift. Day by day, I added another 2½ pounds, and for the first two weeks, the weights were easily lifted.

When the time came to lift 152½ pounds, it again was an easy lift since I had developed a belief that I could easily add 2½ pounds to what I had lifted the day before.  The following day, 155 pounds was again an easy lift.

Keep in mind that during this time I was not working out, but only doing one lift each day.

Eventually, there came a day when I failed to lift the weight. Most likely because I began to doubt my ability to continue the process.  However, I focused my mind on the fact that I had grown in my ability to lift heavier and heavier weights day by day, and resolved to try again the next day.  When it came time to try it again, I was successful.

Over a period of several weeks, I eventually reached the point where I lifted 202½ pounds.  This happened on the last day of the school year, which gave me a tremendous feeling of satisfaction.

Considering that I had performed a single lift each day during the whole experiment, the only possible explanation for the increased ability to lift heavier weights was my belief that I could.

## *Create an Immersion Experience*

Because our minds create associations between things, it is many times easier to change what we believe when we immerse ourselves into a new experience. The new experience allows us to believe in new results.

This can be as simple as kneeling down to pray, or crossing our legs into the lotus position during meditation, or even sitting up straight during a business meeting. The different posture triggers a different set of associations within our minds and allows for a different experience.

Another option is to devote an hour or so to creative daydreaming, creative pretending, or a hypnotic session. When we make the experience unique, we are able to make significantly greater changes within our belief systems.

This idea can be carried further by going to a seminar or retreat center where new beliefs are supported and expected. When you spend several days to several weeks in a new environment, especially one where other people are expressing and living by a different set of beliefs, you are able to immerse yourself even more into the experience and get more out of it.

Some people are able to get many of the same benefits from taking a vacation from their daily lives, either alone or with a loved one. Many of the old stories about saints and wizards living as hermits for a time (or even going on a 40-day vision quest in a remote area), came from people using this concept to help themselves develop more empowering beliefs.

Most of us tend to do better when we can spend time with others who live by the same beliefs we want to develop within ourselves. Going off by ourselves may allow us to break away from those in our daily lives, but it does nothing to help us break away from our habitual thinking and ingrained belief systems. This is why seminars and retreats are better options.

## *Use Additional Sessions*

Although a single belief conditioning session *may* be enough to alter your beliefs and produce the results you desire, you'll probably want to use additional sessions to reinforce the process and alter other beliefs related to your goal.

The ideal frequency for this work seems to be once a day. Multiple sessions per day may work if you have nothing else to do, and are merely passing time. In general, those who do this believe that each session has a limited ability to create change. Anyone who truly expects a single session to be sufficient simply won't feel a need to repeat it.

However, when conditioning sessions are spread too thin, such as once or twice a week, our old habitual thinking patterns can sometimes reverse much of our progress. Considering that a session need not take any more than 10 or 15 minutes, there's no reason sessions cannot be done on a daily basis.

Some people get excellent results doing their belief conditioning work early in the morning, before the day starts, whereas others get good results with afternoon or evening sessions. Some prefer a time before going to sleep each night. Experiment to find what works best for you.

I'm often asked, "How many beliefs should I work on during a single conditioning session? Should I only work on one belief at a time, or can I work on many?" Our minds are wired in such a way to handle 100's and even 1000's of bits of information at a time. We glance at a photo, and our minds process colors, shapes, textures, lighting, and meaning, all in a single moment. In an instant, we interpret the photo as a representation of someone we know, and our minds recall information about this person, and maybe even about the time when the photo was created.

Our minds are capable of processing a lot of information simultaneously, especially when it relates to a single overall concept, like a person, a memory, or a goal. When we have to deal with an unrelated string of information, it's not as easy.

## *Watch For Results*

After you've altered your beliefs about a situation, there's very little left to do except watch for results. They may show up immediately, or you may need to be patient and let things develop over time. The speed of manifestation depends greatly on your beliefs about the process.

You don't want to walk away from your belief conditioning process and immediately ask, "Okay, why hasn't it shown up yet?" Even though such a question indicates a belief in (or at least a desire for) immediate results, it also indicates a belief that the process may not work at all.

Furthermore, you *really* don't want to finish a belief conditioning session with the thought or attitude of "Well, that was a waste of time." As funny as it seems now, you'd be amazed how many people do exactly this. If you find yourself having similar feelings at any point in the process, take it as an indication that you need to work on your beliefs about the process itself and possibly about the power of belief as a whole.

Ideally, the attitude you want to have after working on your beliefs is one of "This is going to be so much fun! I wonder where I'll see results first?" Approaching the whole process as a game with a childlike sense of wonder and curiosity improves the over-all results, and having a genuine expectation of results practically guarantees success.

For most people, especially those just starting to work with these concepts, the best approach is to be open to any and all possibilities. Don't assume that you have to wait, and on the other hand, don't be disappointed if there's no bolt of lightning or choir of angels singing.

## *Follow Your Impulses / Intuition*

Very few of us really expect to see miracles. We would be genuinely surprised to find a pile of money suddenly show up in the middle of our living room, or to have our dream lover knock on our door and propose marriage. If we measure our belief in these things happening, we'll find our level of belief to be below 30%, and quite possibly below 10%. Unless our belief in miracles is over 60%, results of our belief work will usually come through 'normal' processes, such as a raise, a promotion, a new idea, or meeting someone new.

Change is usually created by taking new action. If we insist on doing everything ourselves, we won't be as successful as when we learn to delegate responsibility. In the same way, if we insist on following the same pattern of living, going between work and home and a weekly trip to the same grocery store, then we may be missing the opportunity to meet new people who could help us make the changes we desire.

But doing things differently just for the sake of doing things differently may not be the answer either. Many single people go from bar to bar hoping to meet their next lover, yet they miss many opportunities because they are spending their time in bars instead of places like the library or charitable organizations where many fine singles may be found. (While it is certainly possible to find a wonderful partner in a bar, there's no reason to limit your search for a suitable partner to only one type of establishment.)

No; the right answer is to be in the right place at the right time, doing (and saying) the right thing. We won't always have the ability to know on a conscious level what the right combination may be. Fortunately, we don't have to. By some yet unknown mechanism, the power of belief is able to direct the course of events in such a way that the results we truly expect will actually manifest. All we have to do is allow it to happen.

We can help the process along by paying attention to our impulses, which can guide us to do whatever is necessary to manifest our desired results quickly and easily. Some people call this "intuition," while others differentiate impulses as coming from our 'lower' natures and intuition coming from 'above'. Either way you label it, it's the same thing — an inner prompting that can lead you to your goals if you follow it.

If you notice you're feeling restless and bored, it could be the Universe nudging you along the pathway of your manifestation. If you find yourself feeling curious about a particular person in the parking lot as you put groceries into your car, it could be because that person will be instrumental to your goal, either directly, or by introducing you to someone else. If you start to wonder what would happen if you changed some aspect of your work, that may be a Divine Suggestion opening new doorways of experience.

For example, when I changed my belief about the likelihood of meeting my 'ideal companion', I found myself curious about checking out the local Unity Church. As it turned out, I met my wife there three weeks later. If I hadn't followed my impulses, it wouldn't have happened so quickly.

Some people find a few of their new impulses contradict what they *know* is right, and seem to be leading them to make a fool of themselves. There are two causes for such impulses. The first is a belief that following impulses may be foolish in and of itself. If you believe this, then the belief has opened a doorway to the possibility of foolish behavior. You will want to work on that belief so you may confidently follow your impulses without fear.

The second reason some people find their new impulses contradicting earlier 'knowledge' is because the earlier 'knowledge' is part of the problem being solved. Many times we assume we know something that later proves to be false, like those who believed the Earth was flat. When we can let go of these assumptions, change becomes easier.

I found this to be the case when I changed my beliefs about becoming financially successful. I had tried sales jobs in the past and failed miserably. I tried selling Rainbow vacuums, Omni windows, VIP discount certificates, and free quote appointments for home improvements and failed in all of them. When I created a "not-so-subliminal" tape to help change my money beliefs, I found myself applying for a job with Olan Mills Photography Studios. Although I had been working as a professional photographer, this job required all photographers to also be salespeople.

On the surface, this seemed ludicrous because I 'knew' I couldn't sell if my life depended on it. I 'knew' it was a losing proposition and a sure path to failure. Yet, I trusted my gut and followed the impulse. Although I didn't realize such a thing was possible, I was taught a sales process that was more of a demonstration than a request to make a purchase. It was more of a "Here's what we have to offer" than a "What will it take to make you buy today?" sort of thing. This was something I could see myself doing, and I did quite well with it.

In fact, I did so well I became the number one salesperson in our area. Soon afterwards, I was promoted as a trainer for the local studios, and was given the opportunity to write a weekly newsletter to help the other studios become better at both photography and sales.

None of that would have happened if I hadn't been willing to follow my impulses even when they contradicted what I 'knew' to be the truth.

This example also demonstrates how different beliefs can contradict each other. On one level, I believed I couldn't sell, yet on another level I believed that learning how to sell was possible. One was a Self-Image belief and the other was a World-Level belief. The World-Level belief was stronger, especially after my belief work.

This example also illustrates that the power of belief knows things we don't know ourselves, such as how the Olan Mills sales process was something I could learn and master.

## *Seek Inner Guidance*

Most of us have so many things to focus on that it would almost take a fire alarm to get our attention. Because of this, many of us have lost touch with our intuition and would lose that avenue of guidance unless we do something about it.

Everyone has intuition and can receive guidance from within. 'Women's intuition' is just as common in men as it is in women. All you have to do is relax once in a while (without distractions, if possible) and ask yourself something like, "What should I do now?" and then trust the suggestions that present themselves.

When you relax and clear your mind, you open yourself to the inherent wisdom flowing within each one of us. Where this wisdom comes from has been debated for many generations, and I won't propose an answer here. All that you need to understand is that the wisdom is there and can be tapped into if you believe in it.

Once again, belief is what creates the results you get from everything, including the prompting of your inner wisdom. If you believe you'll only get random thoughts based on past experience when you relax and let ideas bubble forth, then your experience will match your expectation.

However, if you believe that by relaxing and opening yourself up to the flow of the Universe you can receive guidance far beyond your conscious ability to devise, you will experience the joy of psychic visions, or as some religions call them — prophesies.

I remember one of the early times when acting on my inner guidance proved to be far wiser than I would have been on my own. I had just listened to an audio program about developing psychic abilities using compiled material from the Edgar Cayce readings. The recording was a guided meditation that instructed me to visualize myself climbing a mountain to a sacred palace where I would meet someone I trusted completely. Once I met that person, I was to ask him or her a question and listen for the answer.

At the time, I had a friend who was having some difficulty in her marriage and needed some guidance. The question I asked at the end of the guided meditation was something like "What can I do to help my friend?" The answer I received was an image of the two of us going shopping together.

At the time, I was in my early 20's, and like most young men, wasn't inclined to think of shopping as an experience offering any 'real' benefits. As you can imagine, it wasn't exactly a solution I would think of naturally.

When I described the vision to my friend, however, she explained the logic of it to me. Her husband wasn't giving her the attention she needed and having someone share an experience with her, such as shopping, would be a real boost to her self-worth as a person.

So we had a good time going from store to store, looking at a wide variety of things and talking about anything that happened to come up. At the end of the day, I understood her more than ever and learned a valuable lesson about shopping. The wisdom I tapped into knew more than I did consciously, and following my intuition proved to be valuable and worthwhile.

Tapping into your own inner wisdom doesn't require listening to a guided meditation recording, although if such a thing will help, by all means find a good one and use it. The main thing to keep in mind is to relax as completely as possible and allow your mind to turn completely away from the world around you while you tap into the deepest source of wisdom you can access. Once you've reached a place inside that feels right, then ask yourself (even if it's in the guise of a trusted guide and mentor), "What will move me closer to my goals?"

And when you receive an answer — follow your intuition!

## *If Results Are Too Slow*

Whenever I hear someone say that this material doesn't work, I inevitably find they have other beliefs involved which they missed and failed to change. The same has been true with anyone who has not seen results in a reasonable period of time.

Unfortunately, in a book, I am unable to ask pertinent questions to help you discover the specific beliefs involved in your individual situation. While I do offer coaching where we can work together on such issues, it's not for everyone. (Use the contact form at www.PowerKeysPub.com/contact if you want to inquire about personal coaching.)

What I *can* offer here is a suggestion to go through the Belief Archeology process again (page 92) to look for other beliefs relating to your situation. In particular, spend time asking yourself questions like "What's standing in my way?" or "What am I missing?" These questions will help you identify your limiting beliefs and change them.

Don't be too surprised if you find that your limiting beliefs sound a lot like absolute facts, like "I can't get rich because the economy is down right now." or "I can't marry the person I want because they are already married."

When you get answers like these, you need to ask yourself "Why not?" This will reveal the hidden beliefs supporting these statements. For example, no matter how low the economy is, people spend money every day. People started new businesses and became wealthy even during the great depression of the 1930s. If you look hard enough, you'll find someone who has already done what you want to do.

If all else fails, have someone help you. A close friend may be a logical choice, although our friends usually have the same beliefs we do. It's usually better to find someone who is already successful at what you want to do and discuss your beliefs with them.

In Chapter 8, we cover the idea of a "Choose To Believe" MasterMind Group, which can also be of great benefit.

# Chapter 7: Bringing It All Together

T his chapter provides step-by-step examples of how you can implement the concepts and principles described earlier. These examples are only suggestions, and you are welcome to do whatever you feel (and believe) will work best for you.

We will use in our examples a variety of popular goals, such as increasing prosperity, improving relationships, healing bodily conditions, and more. Please note that the associations between goals and processes here are merely arbitrary — you can use *any* process to achieve *any* goal. The most important factor is your beliefs about what will work for you in your particular situation.

Many of the examples in this chapter come from my previous readers and clients, and demonstrate how anyone can simply choose to believe something new and have it become reality.

The first example represents the best suggestion I can give anyone for any goal. This process is simple and direct. The first five steps are foundational and should be used no matter what process you use as a means of altering your beliefs.

## *Example #1: Increasing Prosperity*

### Step 1: Define exactly what you want to achieve.
Small steps are more believable, and are generally easier to obtain. Therefore, if you're currently earning $20,000 per year, it might be a good idea to set an initial goal of $25,000 per year rather than try to produce a million in the next 30 days.

If your ultimate goal is to be a millionaire, break it down into smaller goals, like earning an 'extra' $5000 (not counting your regular income) sometime in the next 3 to 6 months, then set another goal to earn an 'extra' $10,000, and then a third goal to earn an 'extra' $25,000. It's much easier to believe you can earn an 'extra' $5000 than it is to believe you can manifest $1,000,000 all at once. And when you *do* produce the first $5000, the next goal of $10,000 is a lot easier to believe. Once you find yourself earning $25,000 in one shot, then it's a whole lot easier to believe that you can bring in $100,000 the next time around. This is the main reason people say it's a lot easier to earn your second million than it is to earn your first.

Of course, your goal may not be to become a millionaire. Maybe you just want to increase your income to the point where you don't have to worry about paying the bills. Perhaps your goal is to be promoted within your company where you get extra perks and a bigger salary. This is a perfectly acceptable goal, and one many people find much easier to believe.

**Step 2: Consider the various possibilities that could lead to the realization of your goal.**

If your goal is to be promoted, for example, what led to others being promoted in the past? If your goal is to earn $5000 in the next 90 days, how might that be accomplished? (Hint: solving common problems is a good way to wealth.) Knowing how your goal may be realized automatically increases your belief in its possibility, and suggests a visualization to use later.

The easiest way to discover what possibilities exist is to learn from others who have already accomplished the same goal. Ask around at your company and learn what factors generally lead to promotion, especially from your current position to the position you desire. It's much easier to hit an identified target than to shoot blindly in the dark.

There are literally millions of ways to earn money, and many of them can be put to use outside your work hours. Most people work roughly 40 hours per week, leaving 128 hours for other things, like eating, sleeping, and goofing off. If you take your goofing-off time and invest it in a small business pursuit, you'll be surprised to find how easily you can earn a nice side-line income.

I've run a business on the Internet for several years, and every month I learn more ways to generate income with very little time and effort. I've compiled much of this information in my book, *"Treasure Map to Online Riches,"* available on the PowerKeys Publishing website. (www.PowerKeysPub.com)

**Step 3: Further increase your level of belief with creative daydreaming.**

As you go about your normal business, imagine how you would feel once your goal has been achieved. If your goal is to be promoted, then imagine what it would feel like to have increased responsibility and added perks. See yourself as an equal with your current superior and imagine working side by side with him or her rather than as a subordinate. Once you see it in your mind, it feels a lot more natural to expect it in the 'real world'. On a purely physical level, your thoughts will subtly influence your decisions and actions, and this will cause your superiors to respect you more highly, giving you a greater chance of promotion.

If your goal is to increase the profitability of your own business, then imagine what that would be like. Would this be more of the same type of activity you've done in the past? Would it be a new, more profitable activity? Will you have more employees than you do now? Imagine each of the various possibilities and notice how you feel about each one. As you imagine the various possibilities, your feelings will indicate which one is most likely to produce positive results for you.

Pay close attention to your feelings during this step, because your feelings are a good indication of the beliefs involved. If you notice yourself becoming uncomfortable when thinking about having greater responsibility, then spend some time discovering the beliefs responsible for that emotion. If your experience mirrors my own, you may need to first work on your beliefs about your ability to handle responsibility, and work on your beliefs about finances later. Continue to find the responsible beliefs for any other feelings that come up and note them down.

Uncomfortable feelings may come up when your chosen goal is something you've been told you *should* want. In this case, maybe this is the time to reconsider whether this goal is really yours, or if it belongs to someone else. You may want to empower yourself to be true to your own nature rather than submit to a life forced upon you by others.

**Step 4: Measure the strength of your belief that you will actually experience your desired outcome.**

Start out by asking yourself a couple of calibration questions to set your gauge. Use questions to produce both an "absolutely YES" response and an "absolutely NO" response. Now ask yourself a question such as "How much do I believe I will be promoted to the position I want?" or "How much do I believe I will earn an extra $5000 in the next 90 days?"

If the response shows that your belief is at least 70% or more, then you're nearly finished. You may choose to increase it further to make reaching your goal easier, but there's really no need. If the response shows your belief to be less than 50%, then you'll want to improve it.

**Step 5: If you haven't already, now is the time to use the Belief Archeology process (described on page 92) to discover other beliefs involved, and determine which ones need adjusting to support your goals.**

Once you have a list of beliefs to work with, organize them from general to specific (although you may place related belief statements together even when they fit on different levels, as done in the list below), and then work with each one in turn. You'll find some suggested beliefs in Chapter 4: Discover What You Really Believe.

Other beliefs that help attract greater prosperity include:

1. The world gives me the best of everything. All I have to do is be willing to receive it.
2. There is a great abundance of the things I want — they come into my life without effort or thought.
3. Everything I want is already on it's way to me now.
4. Wealth is created by solving problems and entertaining people.
5. The best way to make money is to find a large group of people with a definite need and provide something that meets that need profitably.
6. The more people I serve, the more money I make.

7. The past does not determine the future.
8. The point of Power is here and now.
9. I have the Power to determine the future.
10. Ideas and information are worth much more than labor or possessions.
11. I think clearly and make sound judgments.
12. I can learn and understand anything.
13. I am learning how to be more and more prosperous.
14. I learn from those who know more so that I may duplicate their results.
15. Understanding and wisdom are the foundations upon which I build my world.
16. The only failure is the failure to try.
17. As long as I continue to try, everything that did not work out as expected is only a learning experience.
18. I fulfill a vital function in the world.
19. I have been put on this Earth for a purpose.
20. I am destined for greatness.
21. I am valuable.
22. I am worthy of having everything I want.
23. Abundance is my right.
24. Money is good. I love having money.
25. I enjoy seeing my money grow.
26. Earning money feels good to me.
27. I am getting richer every day.
28. I have more ability than I realize.
29. I am a strong and capable person.
30. I am the center of the universe.
31. The universe is here to serve me.
32. Prosperity is normal and natural in my life.
33. God is very good to me and helps me regularly.
34. I have wonderful talents that create great prosperity.
35. If I don't know something, I can find the information from somewhere or someone.
36. I gladly spend money to learn how to make money.
37. If I can't do a thing, I can hire someone who can do it.

38. I can build a successful business even though I know nothing about it, since I can hire others who do know.
39. As a leader, I earn more money.
40. I can do bigger things with a team.
41. With enough help, I can accomplish anything.
42. I would rather utilize 1% of the efforts of 1000 people than to use 100% of my own efforts.
43. People want to be led; they feel more secure when following a good leader.
44. I am a good leader.
45. I do not allow others to pressure me into doing something I'd rather not do.
46. I prefer to operate with systems in place so that everything is organized and I can be more productive.
47. When unexpected things happen, I ask myself questions like "How can I make this work to my advantage?".
48. If I want something, I do whatever it takes to make it happen.
49. I make sure to have enough money on hand to pay all my expenses ahead of time.
50. The things that frighten me are not as bad as I imagine.

### Step 6: Consciously choose to believe in your goals.

Once again, you are free to choose whatever process you feel will give you the best results. We covered many options in Chapter 5: Choosing New Beliefs.

You may choose to use creative pretending to "try on" a new lifestyle and get comfortable with it. You may use affirmations, affirmative prayer, or pacing and leading affirmations to further condition your mind to believe that what you want will be a natural progression of events in your life. You could use hypnosis to implant these beliefs into a deeper level of your mind, thus making them more powerful and more influential over the circumstances you encounter. Or you could go right to the foundation of your mind and rewrite how these concepts are recorded, making them instantly more believable.

Any of the above processes may be used to directly alter your level of belief in reaching your goals. You could also choose a more indirect approach and use Belief Leverage to alter the reality of your life. With this, you may use anything you believe has the power to change your experience of prosperity (or any other goal you may want to achieve).

For example, you could burn green candles and myrrh incense to attract greater prosperity. You could create a treasure map with pictures of the things you'd like to have in your life. You could write your goal on paper and bury the paper under a tree on the night of the next full moon. While these may seem silly to most modern people, they have been used successfully in ages past and carry the weight of a long tradition.

Other examples include praying to long-deceased saints or the archangels, or even chanting your desires in uncommon languages like Latin, Sanskrit, or one of the many 'angelic' languages. You could even spray your favorite air freshener around your home with the intention that this will attract money into your life. All of these are equally valid *if you believe in them.*

**Step 7: The final step in this process is to accept the fact that you've done enough to have the desired effect.**

The only caveat here is that until you believe that results will instantly appear in front of you, you'll probably have to be physically involved in their manifestation. As they say, you can't win the lottery if you don't buy a ticket.

This means that if you want a promotion, then you may have to ask for it. You may have to take steps to be more promotable, such as taking greater initiative, or coming up with good ideas your company can use to improve sales or cut costs.

How much you have to do to get that promotion depends greatly on what you believe you have to do for it. If you can believe that all you have to do is be in the right place at the right time, then it's quite likely that's all you'll have to do. But even then, you have to be physically involved.

The same is true with the goal of earning an 'extra' $5000 in the next 90 days. If you believe that all it takes is presenting the right idea to the right person at the right time, then you're doing good. Otherwise, most people will find they have to put more effort into the process: researching business ideas, learning a few principles, implementing those principles, and doing a little work.

Whatever work is required, however, you can be sure that it's less now than before you modified your beliefs.

## *Example #2: Improving A Relationship*

**Step 1:   Once again, the first step in any process is to define what you want to accomplish.**

Do you want to find a way to increase cooperation and harmony between you and a coworker?  Do you want to work more closely with your boss to make an impression on him or her as a step towards a raise or promotion?  Are you more interested in gaining the respect of someone you deal with on a regular basis?  Or do you feel the need for romance and adventure with someone special?

As you think about the type of relationship you want to improve, consider why you want this relationship to change.  Do you want to increase cooperation with your coworker because you believe he or she doesn't approve of you?  Or is it because you believe you need their help to achieve other goals, like convincing the boss to lighten up on his or her demands, or having someone to talk to during lunch breaks?  Do you feel a particular person's respect will help you gain a supporter for your cause?  Or do you believe you need their respect to feel good about yourself?

It's quite possible you could find several ways to satisfy these desires, only one of which is to improve the particular relationship at issue.  Allow yourself to consider other possibilities which may exist, and whether any of the alternate possibilities might be a better choice.

For example, if your ultimate goal is to get a raise or promotion, maybe a better option would be to find new ways of saving the company money or increasing sales, or otherwise making yourself more valuable to the company.  Or if your intended goal is to have your spouse support you in a new hobby, and they have no real interest in it, then maybe a better option would be to find a friend who is just as passionate about your hobby as you are, and allow your marriage to continue as it is. There's no requirement for one person to be involved in everything you do, even if that person is your spouse.

The bottom line here is to consider your true objectives and to decide which of several options will best satisfy those objectives.

**Step 2:  In this step, consider the many ways your goal may be realized.**

At this time, don't concern yourself with what is *likely* to happen, but only with what *could* happen.  Do this to help loosen up your beliefs about the situation, and empower yourself to "think outside the box" and consider new beliefs.

For instance, if your previous experience has been that your coworker is shy and doesn't socialize at work, then consider the possibility that something in his or her life may have recently changed and this person now needs someone to talk to.  This would lead him or her to *want* to cooperate with you in a project, such as improving the working conditions in the office.  This possibility would completely eliminate all effort and create an opening so that all you have to do is invite that person to lunch.

As another example, let's say your previous experience has been that almost everyone you've dated has had serious personal issues, then consider the possibility that there are hundreds of perfectly compatible partners right within your own neighborhood, and you could meet one at any moment.  This was my own situation and the possibility I chose to believe a short time before I met my wife, Linda.  Choosing to believe in what initially seemed to be a ridiculous possibility led to a wonderfully enjoyable result.

What ridiculous possibility would make the realization of your goal seem like a miracle?

**Step 3: Boost the strength of your belief that your goal will be easily achieved with creative daydreaming.**

Most of us have trouble believing that life can be easy because we've experienced more difficulty than we cared to encounter. We have many memories about working hard to accomplish our goals, about others not cooperating with us, or simply rejecting us for one reason or another. To shift our belief around to the point where we fully expect others to accept us and cooperate, we usually need to create more memories of better experiences.

Have you ever heard this expression: "the subconscious mind cannot tell the difference between reality and a vividly imagined experience"? This is why creative daydreaming works as well as it does, because it allows you to create memories of your own choosing, which support whatever you choose to believe.

By daydreaming about what you'd like to experience, you are building a belief that you will actually have that experience. You begin to expect your desired outcome more than you did before. And when you have enough vivid memories of gaining the cooperation of others, or being accepted the way you want to be, you start to find yourself *expecting* cooperation and acceptance in your daily life.

We all know at least one person who spends a lot of time daydreaming with nothing to show for it. The things they daydream about never become real in their lives. I want to address this situation, because the reason for it is very important to understand.

It comes down to a single idea. The core idea we've been discussing throughout this whole book — belief. If we believe that our daydreams will have no influence in our physical lives, then they won't. But if we understand the power of belief itself, and realize that our daydreams are helping to condition those beliefs, which will be reflected in the world around us, then we have opened the doorway for those daydreams to become real.

Although we may have heard that daydreaming is a waste of time, let's consider the possibility that those who said it did not understand the tremendous power of belief, and were not aware of what daydreaming can accomplish. Let's choose to believe the scientific evidence showing our beliefs have the power to instantly and dramatically alter the physical world around us, and allow ourselves to take advantage of this power to make our lives more enjoyable.

The process itself can be wondrously enjoyable. Imagining others as excited about cooperating with us, accepting us for who we are, and even anxious to spend time with us can be very enjoyable indeed, and even empowering. Feelings of warm acceptance and personal validation grow strong when we daydream creatively about the possibilities that could exist in our relationships. Seeing our boss take pride in our accomplishments, and hearing him or her praise us in front of the other employees fills a deep inner need within each of us just as surely as eating a sumptuous meal fills our bellies.

Creative daydreams involving romance and adventure can be even more fulfilling, as they can easily become very vivid and intense. The feeling of excitement evoked within our daydreams is recorded as a strong memory supporting a powerful belief that we will have similar experiences in our real lives.

**Step 4: Now is the time to take stock of your current beliefs and find out which beliefs support your goal and which ones need to be adjusted.** (In this example, we are combining steps 4 and 5 from the prosperity example.)

Ask yourself a short series of calibration questions, like "Do I believe that I know my own name?" or "Do I believe that I live on planet Earth?" or "Do I believe that 2+2=73?" to set both ends of the measuring gauge. Next, ask yourself if you believe that you will reach your goal in a reasonable amount of time. Notice the level of your belief.

Continue by using the Belief Archeology process to discover beliefs which may be limiting your expectations of reaching this goal. Ask yourself questions such as "What's standing in my way?" and "Why can't I have what I want in this situation?" The answers to these types of questions will reveal your limiting beliefs, which you now know how to change.

Take your list of limiting beliefs and rewrite them as you would like them to be. Here is a list of beliefs that have been successfully used by others to improve their relationships:

1.  The world is a beautiful place where dreams come true.
2.  The past does not determine the future.
3.  I can create a future containing everything I desire.
4.  Relationships are a celebration of life.
5.  Everyone is equal in the eyes of God.
6.  I am neither better nor worse than any other person.
7.  I am worthy of having wonderful relationships.
8.  Relationships come easily into my life.
9.  My relationships usually grow very deep, very quickly.
10. I am completely satisfied and fulfilled from within.  My relationships are merely a bonus to me, richly enjoyed.
11. I accept myself for being who and what I am.  I'm okay just the way I am.
12. Other people accept me for who I am.
13. There are thousands of people who would enjoy being in a relationship with me.
14. The more I value myself, the more others value me.
15. I am a constantly evolving being.
16. It is my destiny to be happy and fulfilled.
17. I get anything and everything I want.
18. I get a lot of value out of every relationship I have; either from the experience itself or something I gain as a result.
19. Meeting new people is wonderfully exciting.
20. I enjoy meeting new and interesting people every day.
21. People are generally kind and considerate of others.
22. People usually respond with love and acceptance.
23. People like me.
24. I enjoy being with others.
25. People enjoy being around those who like people.
26. People respond to those they enjoy being around.

27. It's okay for people to have different opinions and desires.
28. People respond to me because I like them and let them be whomever they choose to be without judgment.
29. People feel a need for acceptance and companionship.
30. People are motivated by their own interests, not mine.
31. People become more interested in those who first show an interest in them.
32. The more I value the opinions of others, the more they are willing to cooperate with me.
33. The more I understand what people want, the more I can easily motivate them to cooperate with me.
34. I don't need to completely understand another person.
35. I don't need another person's compliance to be valuable.
36. The more I recognize the Divinity within each person I meet, the more blessed my relationships become.
37. The more I act towards others with love, the more love is reflected in the faces of those I meet.
38. I am willing to take whatever steps are necessary to improve all of my relationships.
39. The love I radiate outward comes back to me multiplied many times over.
40. The more I strive to understand others, the more they are willing to understand me.
41. People want my approval and are willing to give me what I want in exchange for it.
42. People feel good in my presence and are willing to do almost anything to be with me.
43. People will accept constructive criticism (a suggestion for improvement) if they've been praised beforehand.
44. People are more willing to admit fault to someone who does the same.
45. "Getting even" is a sure pathway to trouble.
46. Violence may command respect, but never love.
47. Throwing a tantrum will never make someone love me.
48. I do not allow others to pressure me into doing something I'd rather not do.

49. The things that frighten me are not as bad as I imagine.
50. No one wants to harm me in any way.

**Step 5: This step is where you consciously alter your beliefs to support your goals.**

Once again, you are free to choose whatever process you feel will give you the best results. For demonstration purposes, I will describe two different processes anyone can use to attract a new romantic relationship.

One process is to record yourself speaking a list of affirmations relating to your goal, and to play this recording in the background of everything you do. I call this the "not-so-subliminal" approach because the affirmations may be clearly heard if you pay attention to the recording, yet will have the same effect as subliminal messages when you focus on other activities, such as driving, doing your work, watching TV, or sleeping.

The more your inner mind hears the ideas being expressed on the recording, the more the ideas seem normal and natural, and thus the more believable they become.

When you hear a voice in the background constantly telling you that you are a desirable person, or that many people respect you and follow your lead, eventually you start to believe it and expect responses of this nature from others. And when you expect a particular response, you tend to get it more often than not.

A recording like this can be made more effective in two ways. First, you can relax your body and mind to the point where you go into a hypnotic trance and become more suggestible. This helps the suggestions reach a deeper level of your mind where they are more powerful and produce stronger results. And second, you can mentally respond to each suggestion with the thought "yes, that's right." This adds impact to each suggestion and communicates to your inner mind that you fully support the ideas you hear.

Another process, which works exceptionally well when your goal is to attract a new romantic relationship is to use creative pretending to act out the desired experience.

Some people do this naturally. They go out on dates with friends and pretend that they are with the love of their life. When they look at their friend's face, they mentally 'see' the face of someone they would like to be involved with. When they sit next to their friend, they imagine it is their desired lover they feel nearby.

This can be taken further if your friend is willing. I once had a close friend who was romantically interested in me, and although I didn't feel the same way about her, I allowed the relationship to become intimate at one point. Before doing so, I made sure she understood that the evening was to be a one-time thing, and I didn't want to lead her on to think our relationship could be anything more than friendship.

During the evening, I imagined I was with my "dream lover" and had several specific things in mind I wanted to be a part of the future relationship. To make a long story short, over the course of the next few months, I ended up meeting someone, and the relationship was 90% of everything I had visualized during the creative pretending process.

As a side-note, I can say I've used the creative pretending process in a number of other situations, including the receiving of material possessions without a lot of cost or effort. I've already described bringing vehicles into my life through this process, and there have been several other cases as well.

Creative pretending is a lot of fun and powerfully effective, especially when you understand the power of belief and how pretending can condition and activate your beliefs.

**Step 6: At this stage of the process, the only thing left to do is watch for the manifestation.**

Once more, unless you truly *expect* instant results, you'll probably have to be personally involved in the manifestation of your goal. This means you may have to take the first step and introduce yourself to someone new, or be the one to offer a hand in friendship. If you're working to correct an acrimonious relationship, you may find the turnaround to be a gradual process.

If you find yourself hesitant about taking the first step, this may be an indication that one or more beliefs still need to be worked on, such as your belief about what is appropriate, or your belief about yourself as an outgoing individual.

In relationships, it is important to follow your intuition and seek inner guidance often. Although it's not necessary to believe in a spiritual connection with others, having such a belief tends to improve our relationships in many ways.

## *Example #3: Increased Health and Vitality*

This case history comes from one of the original founders of the Unity movement, Myrtle Filmore, and is in her own words. (Used by permission of Unity, www.unityonline.org.)

"I myself was once an emaciated little woman, upon whom relatives and doctors had placed the stamp 'T.B.' [tuberculosis]. And this was only one of the ailments— there were others considered beyond any help, except possibly the changing of structures through an operation. There were family problems too. We were a sickly lot, and came to the place where we were unable to provide for our children. In the midst of all this gloom, we kept looking for the way out, which we felt sure would be revealed. It was!

"The light of God revealed to us—the thought came to me first—that life was of God, that we were inseparably one with the source, and that we inherited from the divine and perfect Father. What that revelation did to me at first was not apparent to the senses. But it held my mind up above the negation, and I began to claim my birthright and to act as though I believed myself the child of God, filled with His life. I gained. And others saw that there was something new in me.

"I knew that God, whom I could call Father, would not create imperfect children. As I thought of it, I began to realize that I was truly God's child, and that because of this I must of necessity inherit from Him. Then ... I saw that the life that is in us is the life of God. Therefore, I reasoned, the plan of God must be an inherent part of the mind of man. ... I began to live with God, and to talk with Him. ...

"God revealed to me that my body was intelligent; that I could direct and praise it, and it would respond. ... He was giving me His life, substance, and intelligence, and I was to use them, even more freely than I had used the blessings my Earthly father had given me. ...

"I went to all the life centers of my body and spoke words of Truth to them—words of strength and power. I asked their forgiveness for the foolish, ignorant course that I had pursued in the past, when I condemned them and called them weak, inefficient, and diseased.

"I did not become discouraged at their being slow to wake up, but kept right on, both silently and aloud, declaring the words of Truth, until the organs responded. And neither did I forget to tell them that they were free, unlimited Spirit. I told them ... that they were not corruptible flesh, but centers of life and energy omnipresent. ...

"I promised [the Father] that I would never, never again retard the free flow of that life through my mind and my body by any false word or thought; that I would always bless it and encourage it with true thoughts and words in its wise work of building up my body temple; that I would use all diligence and wisdom in telling it just what I wanted it to do.

"I also saw that I was using the life of the Father in thinking thoughts and speaking words, and I became very watchful as to what I thought and said.

"I did not let any worried or anxious thoughts into my mind, and I stopped speaking gossipy, frivolous, petulant, angry words.

"You ask what restored me to vigorous health. It was a change of mind from the old, carnal mind that believes in sickness to the Christ Mind of life and permanent health. 'Be ye transformed by the renewing of your mind.' 'As he thinketh within himself, so is he.' I applied spiritual laws effectively, blessing my body temple until it manifested the innate health of Spirit. These wonderful laws will work for you too when you apply them diligently and in faith."

What I want you to notice in this case history is the use of logic, starting from core Universal Beliefs and working towards a more personal surface belief in health and healing. In the Unity faith, as in many New Thought systems, it is believed that statements of health and healing are stronger than statements of illness and disease. This is one reason they stress the use of 'Truth Statements' in the treatment of conditions. It is also a beneficial belief making changes easier to manifest.

## *Example #4: Healing of Psoriasis*

The power to heal extends beyond mere cuts and bruises, illnesses and diseases. It extends into areas many consider hereditary and unchangeable, such as psoriasis. Here is a case history showing how healing of such a condition can happen with a simple decision.

"It was in my early teens that I was diagnosed with psoriasis. It began in my scalp and then slowly appeared on my elbows, shins, knees and left hand.

"I have read many books on the topic and sought advice from numerous general physicians, dermatologists, naturopaths and alternative healers. I tried steroidal creams, light therapy, all kinds of supposedly miracle cure formulas, changed my diet, lost weight, exercised and meditated but all to no avail.

"I felt defeated in the belief that psoriasis was, as stated by the allopathic industry, a hereditary, non-curable skin disorder.

"My wardrobe consisted of long sleeved shirts, pants and the odd long skirt. For over 20 years, Summer has been a dreaded season. Outdoor fun was simply not in my vocabulary.

"About a year ago, there began a new voice within me and day after day the conversation with this new, inner entity took up more and more of my mental focus.

"This inner voice whispered that there was something out there waiting for me. Something that involved a deeper connection to myself and the world around me. It spoke of change. It spoke of deeper happiness. It spoke of health.

"After about six months of introspection, I could not ignore this intuitive dialog anymore.

"After working over 18 years in my chosen field, and to the surprise of pretty much everyone I knew, I sold my truck, gave notice at the cute-as-a-button cabin that I was renting and handed in my resignation at work.

"'To do what' you may ask? Well, I joined my love, now my fiancé, on his 32 foot sailboat. We are currently discovering the coast of British Columbia, Canada.

"Along with my decision to go sailing, I also decided to believe in trusting my inner thoughts and most importantly, I began to believe in my body's ability to heal itself.

"Here's the kicker. It's been around six months now since I made my lifestyle change and, so far, around 70% of my psoriasis has healed!

"When moored, we both pick up part time work. Otherwise, I write, journal, read and study. I am expressing my true self more than I ever have in my life."

There are several ways to interpret this case history reported by S.C. Patience. You could say her decision to trust her body's ability to heal itself led to the healing of her skin condition, or you could say the change in lifestyle had something to do with it. Either way, it was a belief that life could be better which led her to make the lifestyle change, and thus her ultimate healing.

## *Example #5: True Love*

The following is a great case history for a number of reasons. It deals with beliefs on several levels, including beliefs about the process of changing beliefs.

"I was one of the many people who once believed that all men are the same. They are all users, liars, abusers, and basically game players. Every time I met someone, I put up my guard because I truly believed that they were like the person before them. They would eventually wind up hurting me. I never trusted them because they weren't really trustworthy. They were the kind of men that I would not wish on my worst enemy. I had men who were physically, emotionally and verbally abusive. Emotionally distant as well. Just not the kind of guys that I would want to spend the rest of my life with, let alone spend too much time with them. But I continued to (unconsciously) seek out these types of men, somehow believing that one of these days I would find the right man for me.

"I decided that enough was enough. I started reading a lot of material from self help books. Audio cassettes, and CD's. I learned that your thoughts create your reality. I also did research on the Internet regarding 'affirmations'.

"I felt that something had to give and I had to do something or else nothing would change. I did not want to live a life of loneliness, though I much preferred that to what I was getting. I started reciting affirmations in the morning, on my breaks at work, and on my way home. Basically asking the Universe for the type of man that I desired.

"After about 6 to 8 months, I went on a dating site, and had a very good response from someone who I am now in a serious relationship with. We have been together for almost one year and he loves me for who I am and is who I consider to be my "soul mate." He is everything I asked for and more. We will be getting married in the near future. Now, I am working on the financial part.

"It was not easy, it took awhile for things to change. In the beginning it felt awkward. As a matter of fact, my mind refused to make any positive changes due to years of negativity. The affirmations and my subconscious were at constant war, day in and day out. But after what I read about affirmations and how your mind will not readily accept changes so easily, I persisted. My mind kept telling me: 'Come on now, you know this stuff doesn't work! Who are you kidding! All men are the same!' Then it would retrieve the negative and abusive relationships of the past as examples of why affirmations won't work. After doing extensive research on the Internet about your 'subconscious mind', and knowing that it would reject any positive changes, I continued to repeat them. As often as I could.

"After awhile, it became easier and easier for my mind to accept what it was hearing from my own voice. I would say them aloud most times. It was only then that

I relaxed a little, I started believing that there was someone out there who would truly love me and treat me the way I deserved to be treated. That's when I decided to look into the dating site.

"I now know that you don't have to live your life in misery, loneliness and settle for anything you don't want. I am still growing and learning, but I will get there. I have never been happier."

Barbara K. found that the past did not determine the future, and she could experience a relationship which was completely different from anything she had known before. Her progress took longer than it had to because of her beliefs about the process, however, she was able to choose to believe in true love, which is now evident in her life.

## *Example #6: General Prosperity*

Here is a beautiful example of how dramatically a life can be changed through the power of belief. In this example, you'll notice how Caterina kept her mind occupied with positive thoughts as a process to change what she believed was possible in her life. Once the beliefs changed, her world reflected the new beliefs back to her.

"Before using the power of belief my situation was, let's say, dying or actually, I felt dead. Lonely, unhappy, full of grief, anger, jealousy and bad thoughts of myself and others. I was struggling through a divorce with two small children, no money, a poor job and no moral help from anyone, BUT MYSELF!!

"In order to change the situation, I started looking straight within myself, asking myself questions. Reading plenty of self-help books and keeping in line with excellent, really excellent websites, that have helped me stay upright and use techniques that have helped me find a new me. My mind was the greatest tool. I visualized day by day and BELIEVED that all would come as wished, hoped, prayed. I used my mind and strength in the right manner and ALL was just the way I believed. I started changing for the better.

"The changes that occurred were magnificent: I started saying positive words to myself, to others. I felt strong and constant, I started working out every single morning, my bad habits disappeared. The bad people just disappeared from my life and I started meeting the most wonderful humans of my life. The person I fell in love with (that at first ignored me) came back with the best feeling. I found an excellent job, and most of all I became the most loving, caring and strong hearted MOTHER of my two spectacular children!!

"Let me say that the whole process took me a very long time. It began, I guess 3 years ago. The questions I asked myself were plain and simple, but very difficult to face and answer, such as 'Who do you think you are? What are you expecting from life? Why do people react to you in a certain way? How responsible am I? How powerful can I be? What is life really about?'

"Let's say I was facing the birth of a brand new me. The answers I'd give to myself were just really taking all my confusion out, releasing me from negative thoughts, and making me understand how my words were not clear.

So, really, asking and answering was really a way of having the courage to face my own truths and all the corrections that had to be made in order to become the person I was seeking in others. That was part of the process of giving birth to myself, difficult BUT amazingly beautiful."

## *Example #7: Home Ownership*

"I was raised to 'believe' that single women didn't buy homes for themselves — they waited until a man married them and bought a home together or moved into the man's home. I moved to Los Angeles, California in 1985 at the age of 32 and rented a home for $950 a month in the Mar Vista district near Marina Del Rey. Within two years I started to feel I wanted to own my own home, but still had no husband. I had three strikes against me — I was single, I was a woman, and I was self-employed.

"I used visualizations — and going to the open houses helped me to feel more and more like it was possible for me to own a home — and once I started placing offers, even when they were rejected — I was visualizing that for the right home for me, my offer would be accepted and it eventually was. Also, I changed my own self-talk. Instead of agreeing that a single woman really couldn't own a home as I was taught to believe, I started telling myself — 'the right home is out there for you.' I think what was key for me was recognizing that the belief I grew up with didn't fit me anymore and I made the decision to believe just the opposite, then took inspired action.

"I started to attend open houses, learn about the market and go to different areas of the city. I was disappointed to find out I couldn't afford in the area I was renting in, so I expanded my search and went looking in the San Fernando Valley. On July 4th of 1987, a realtor left an American flag with his business card on my front lawn, and I kept it. I contacted him in the Spring of 1988 and, God bless him, he was willing to work with me. He went with me to open houses, answered my questions, put bids on several properties, none of which were accepted.  But neither 'Bob' nor I gave up.

"Eventually my bid of $132,000 was accepted on a single-family 2-bedroom home in the San Fernando Valley, and today my home has a market value of over $450,000.  I have been able to refinance twice to cover bills when my copywriting work was slow and even helped my sister consolidate her debt.

"Owning a home has helped me to view myself as a prosperous person who takes good care of herself.  I would still like to have a man to share life with, but will always be proud of the fact that I changed the belief I was raised with and forged ahead to become a single, female, still self-employed homeowner!!"

In this example, Dee Long of Van Nuys, California, focused on visualizations and going to open houses to reinforce her chosen belief that she could own her own home.  Once she made the conscious choice to believe in herself, the world around her supported her new beliefs and responded by leading her to the realization of her goal.

## *Example #8: Business Success*

"Times were tough, I'd just had my second child and was tired, I didn't want to return to accounts.  I had been on the Internet when I came across my dream job — it combined all my natural talents — perfect I thought.  I signed up to the network marketing company and business was not going as I'd expected.  I was doing the work, contacting people, talking to people and I had even got an amazing product result, however the big checks were not coming my way.

"What did I know about my field?  Everyone around me was progressing but who would want to talk to me?

I was a lot younger than those around me and I didn't know anyone. I looked around and decided that I just didn't make the grade, I could never run my own business. I had no products left for my clients and I had spent all the money on clearing my debts.

"Sadly in August of this year (2007) my mother died from heart disease at 55. This came as a total shock. She was not even slightly over weight but had smoked and drank. However, I sat at home before the funeral and decided that I was in control of my own life. Mum had always taught me to follow my dreams and never give up.

I got out a piece of paper and wrote down my goal. By closing my eyes and dreaming, I made a clear picture of my bank account, my house, my family and my work. Once I knew where I wanted to be, I set to work on finding out how I was going to get there.

This lead me to making a list of all the things my current job (of only 6 weeks) did to help me get towards my goal. Invoicing for a big, plastic-bucket company getting next to nothing an hour was not high on the goal route planner. I spent many nights focusing on me — a self-audit of all my good points, things people say to me, what I enjoy doing and how I felt. I made a list of all the positive and negative things. Once I knew which of these qualities and beliefs were holding me back, I focused on their positive side. I rewrote each one and one per night before I went to bed I picked one and would say it over and over in the new positive form until I truly believed it.

"What all this made me realize was that the network marketing company I had been involved in previously was just what I was looking for. With my new positive mindset I worked on my attitude and as if by magic the phone started to ring again. People were ringing me for appointments and the check added another '0'!

By working on myself and what prevented me from achieving my goals I now know just what I need to do to go forward. All the actions I take within my business are in line with my end goal. I keep myself organized and every night practice my positive affirmations. I have just recently (last week) qualified to the next level on my marketing plan, which in itself is amazing for me — and all this because I worked on me — and what I believe I can do!

"Losing my mother tore my world apart. I am an only child so I had to support my father. What all this work on myself also taught me was that it's OK to look forward, that grief is not to be feared. Sad times are already, for me, replaced with reflection. My mother was a wonderful woman and I am so proud to be her daughter. I stood up at the funeral and spoke the poem I had written for her without a quiver in my voice, I was able to do this because I told myself I would. The 400 friends and family at the funeral all made comments about how wonderful the service was. Without the work I was doing on myself I could have never had done it."

Lucy Thornton found that daydreaming about what she wanted helped her get clear on the right pathway to take to get there. She also found that as her beliefs in herself and the work she was doing improved, so did the results she received from her work. In addition, she also found that success in one area will boost your confidence in your ability to handle other situations as well.

## *Example #9: Dream Car*

"Prior to changing my mindset I had fixed my eyes on my dream car, only to realize it was too expensive for me to afford and I probably would never have one. My children knew it was my dream car since every time I would see one I would say, 'there's mommy's dream car!' I had even found the same model and color I wanted in a matchbox-size car and kept it on my desk. I would tell myself that someday I would have the life-size version.

"What really made me determined to change the way I thought about this is twofold. First, I was telling myself it was a dream car and that kept it from becoming a reality. Second, and life changing, my daughter told me she was riding in her dad's car and saw my dream car and automatically, out of reaction, exclaimed and pointed that she just saw mommy's dream car!! Her dad (we are not married) told her she needs to stop saying things like that, because unless mommy has that kind of money laying around it won't be happening. My daughter was devastated that our dream game was squashed. That moment is when I decided I needed to make this a reality.

"I really didn't do much. My thoughts turned from dreaming to not wanting to damage my child's own ability to dream and make things happen. I think my change happened on an unconscious level that made me more determined and attracted this to me.

"One day, I happened to open the paper to the car classified, which I never normally did, and saw my dream car listed in the used car section. I had been going to dealerships previously and knew they were still out of my budget and was just waiting for them to come down more in price. So as I read the classified ad, I noticed the price seemed too low, and that made me call the seller. Come to find out, it was the correct price, lower than bluebook, yet a steal of a car! I called my bank, and was afraid they would still tell me it's too much, but instead they told me to go pick it up. I'm still driving this car today, and I absolutely love it!

"I think that this event not only changed the way I think, but also others. I can tell you that when I drove home in this car — in the color I had dreamed of having — something short of a miracle happened with my children's attitude. I just showed them that dreams CAN happen and their faces were lit up as if I just performed magic!

"It was all about putting your mind to it.

"Oh, and yes, I did feel great pleasure the first time I pulled up to my ex's home when picking up my daughter and seeing his face in shock as to what I was driving."

This case history shows how Jonna, like most of us, responds more to the fear of loss than the desire for gain. When faced with the prospect of damaging her child's ability to dream, she made an unconscious decision to make her own dream real. And once she made her decision — and believed it would happen — she was naturally guided to find what she wanted at a price she could afford.

## *Example #10: Stepping out in Faith*

"My name is Debra Kochin. I work as an order-taker and dining room attendant at Wendy's Restaurant. My husband and I are mutually separated and I am trying to fend for myself. My mom helps me by allowing me to live with her.

"I have attended Unity Church of Peace for two years, and have found a new family here. I also found the tools to overcome my defeats and fears.

"Recently, I attended the Edwene Gains Prosperity seminar. I went because someone at church recommended going. During the seminar, Edwene proclaimed that the windows of heaven will open and pour out

blessings upon you if you would only practice three
things:

    1. Tithe 10% of your earnings to your spiritual
    source of nourishment.

    2. Forgive everyone everyday

    3. Imagine being the person you want to be, the
    job you want to have, the home you want to
    own, the car you want to drive, the places you
    want to visit, etc. every morning when you get
    up.

"At the end of the seminar an offering was being
taken. Was I really going to get serious and apply these
principles? I better write a check. (Gulp.) Could I really
forgive my bosses, my grown children, and thoughtless
friends every day? (Gulp.) Can I change the horrible
black and white gritty images of me being homeless,
wandering through the Heartside area of Grand Rapids?
And how was I going to sustain full color images of
being in a classroom of eager young faces teaching them
how to draw? How could I possibly believe that the
image of me closing the wrought iron gate of my
Victorian home, BMW keys in my hand, could possibly
come true? I am fifty-five years old with no vocational
training, and my middle-aged slipping brain is working
against me. I also was homeless before, so all these
bleak images keep slipping into the positive movie that
I'm trying to create. However, even though these
negatives keep popping up, I still persist in picturing
forgiveness, acceptance, and the most joyous dream for
my future, even if only for a few moments each
morning.

"The first week I applied these principles my hours at
work doubled. I made a new friend at the Edwene
Gaines seminar, and she now attends our church
regularly and is a joy to be with. I sold one of my
paintings at a charity auction. My general manager has

asked for my input on how to grow our sales volume, and openly declared how much she enjoys working with me. Friends and family and church members are cheering me on in my artistic endeavors, and if this wasn't all, the window of heaven literally did open up.

"On Saturday, November 3$^{rd}$, a legal size manila envelope arrived by registered mail for me. {What in the world could it be?} I eagerly opened it. It was from Gordon Foods! I had applied for a job there four years ago but never heard from them. Bemused, thinking it's about time they contacted me, the contents of this letter blew me away. I and untold other women had been discriminated against and a legal suit involving the federal government versus Gordon Foods had been resolved with a settlement to be divided between all female applicants who had applied for the warehouse position from 2003 to 2007. Furthermore, the settlement would be in the form of wages, so withholding of social security and taxes would be involved. {Back wages?} {Since 2003!} WOW! At the time of this printing I have not heard the outcome of this wild proclamation, however, the fact that God remembered me and that the universe is conspiring to help me is truly awe-inspiring. God *does* love me and his eye is on the sparrow after all. Maybe those negative thoughts aren't the truth after all.

"This is a story of faith the size of a mustard seed. Practice, {that means it doesn't come instantly} affirmations and visualizations, no matter how fearful and depressed you are, and forgive even when your heart is as hard as stone at the moment, and give because the universe will give right back to you {pressed down and overflowing} and thank and recognize the Lord our God."

## *Example #11: Inner Strength*

Sometimes, the results we seek aren't so much material as they are psychological, such as peace of mind or a feeling of strength. In this case study, you'll see how Jan Burd's belief in prayer led to inner peace even in the midst of crisis.

After two years of illnesses in the family, and five deaths that affected me deeply, including the 14-month journey with cancer that my 20-year-old grand-daughter lived, I came to a point where I felt I absolutely could not go on feeling the way I was.

Along with the feeling of grief overwhelming me at times, I had come to realize that I thought losing Heather at twenty-one was the hardest challenge I would ever have.

Heather, my granddaughter, made her transition five months ago. Although I have great faith about Heather's consciousness now, and how incredibly happy she is, my family consists of human beings.

The hardest journey, I now believe, is watching my daughter grieve for her daughter and, as a mother, be able to do absolutely nothing to help her. As well as Terri, I also have the rest of Heather's family (including me) to find a way to go through this experience.

I have deep faith, but try telling your daughter that it is God's will that Heather passed so young, she's in a better place, it's all part of a bigger picture, and at the same time hold on to those beliefs yourself.

I am the office manager in my church, and on a Saturday evening, I was at my job finishing up for Sunday service. I was so overcome with the feeling of not seeing any way to lift myself from the increasing depression I had been feeling, I went to the sanctuary where I cried and wailed. I began talking to Creative

Source and said, "God, I can't do this anymore. I don't know what to think, say, feel, or do."

I also realized I did not even know HOW to release it and turn it over to the Higher Source, and I expressed this verbally.

I said, "I need you to take this from me because I need to find a way to living a peaceful life as I am going through this lesson. I don't know how to do that right now, please help me." I begged, but still had no idea what to do.

My life, at this moment, felt like total hell. I am normally an appreciative person who honors everything in life, but I couldn't now.

I finished my work and went home crying all the way. I continued to talk to God in the short time before going to sleep. Crying, begging, pleading, feeling completely desolate.

The prayer I went to sleep with in my mind and on my lips was, "Please help me. I don't know how to surrender and really need intervention. I love you, and I know you are always there for me — it feels as I have lost you, I need help." Over and over, I prayed this plea.

The next morning, when I awakened after a night of fitful sleep, the first words that came into my head were, "DIVINE INTERVENTION COMES, AND I AM FREE."

At that moment I felt as if a weight had been lifted off my shoulders.

I realized that Source Energy had been with me for weeks leading up to this surrender, and that knowledge gave me so much comfort.

A few weeks before, as I was driving somewhere, I remembered a CD by Mark Stanton Welch I have. I got it at an "Adults of Unity" conference four years before, loved it, but had not listened to it for about three years.

When I played it, I loved it so much again. I kept it in my CD player and played it whenever I was in my car.

When these things happen to me, I know they have meaning of some sort,  but was really unaware just how significant it was to become to me.

In one of his songs was the line, "Divine intervention comes and I am free.  I am free, I am free ................ just let go and love will find the way."

Am I without the challenges?  No.  But I don't feel as if I'm doing this alone, ever.  Do I feel grief?  Yes.  But I know I don't have to bear it alone.  I am a pretty fast learner, and this experience has shown me surrender.  I will not let it go so long the next time I need help.

I realize that I also released the idea that I have to always have the answer — an idea that had taken root in me during the past two years, not in my whole life experience, just as far as my family and friends.

I now go to prayer first, not after I have tried to solve the problem.

## *Example #12: Peace of Mind*

"I was working as the COO of a hospital for a large healthcare company that was very financially successful, but had a history of chewing up its best staff and spitting them out — badly mangled if still alive.  The company skirts the edges of ethical conduct in the name of profits and rewards good old boys (and girls), and cutthroat-ism over ethics and competency.

"I reevaluated my life, looked at my values and decided that I'd rather give up the security, prestige and pay in exchange for peace of mind and leading an authentic life.  Friends, colleagues and family alike discouraged me and warned me I would not be able to find another job 'at your age'.

"I meditated, prayed and got the answer to 'do it and trust'. Since then, I have expanded my old love for writing and speaking. I have delivered keynote addresses in places as diverse as Birmingham, AL and Council Bluffs, IA. I have received all-expense paid invitations to speak in the beautiful Virgin Islands and the breathtaking Waikiki in Hawaii.

"Meanwhile, I cannot keep up with requests for writing projects. I had been diagnosed as diabetic in 2004. I have since run a 5K race, my blood sugar is normal without medication and I have a sense of peace.

"I have not practiced clinical lab science for over 13 years, but when I needed a job, I applied and was hired by a local hospital. Like riding a bike, I fell right back in line without missing a beat. My skills appeared as I need them. Although my former colleagues see this as a demotion, I am grateful that God is working a miracle through me every day. And I am getting paid for it!

"Best of all are the day-to-day miracles. I seem to get parking spaces right next to buildings; I contemplate a decision, ask for a sign and suddenly look out a window and see bright pink blossoms on an azalea bush surrounded by drought-racked plants.

"I have long been a 'new-ager' since I discovered a Unity church on a 'random walk' as a teenager. I went in, listened, got some literature, and immediately felt at home. This was like joining a cult according to the more traditional members of my family.

"The crisis of conscience with that healthcare company forced me to confront my beliefs and commit to really 'walk the walk'. I learned all over again to have a constant dialog with God and to be grateful each and every day. I came to the realization that my gratitude was a conscious decision, even 'regardless of', or 'despite'. I had always been grateful 'for' something. I felt such power and relief when I committed to being grateful and 'OK' each and every day regardless of appearances. This was both a revelation and a relief — not to mention a huge reward.

"I wake up each day deciding to be happy and eager to experience what's 'out there'. Far from being idealistic, Pollyanna-ish or fatalistic, this is a way of life, a philosophy with huge pay offs.

"Just the other day, I went in for a colonoscopy because of some bleeding. Of course I was concerned, but I was also optimistic and curious. I met the most amazing people leading up to the procedure. The growths they found were noncancerous and I was put on a course of a new anti-inflammatory drug. A few short weeks later, my amazing gastroenterologist repeated my scope and is still in shock as to how fast the growths shrunk. I am obviously grateful, but not shocked.

"Since we can entertain only one thought and feeling at a time, making a commitment to be resilient and in a state of joy means that I have already won. I start each day ahead of the game. The part of this I am truly amazingly grateful and humbled about is how my daily life is sprinkled with little miracles each day. Another big bonus is that my sense of detachment from any one specific outcome frees me up to enjoy life and in an almost ironic twist, the specific trappings of wealth, happiness (that I no longer desperately crave) often fall in my lap. How amazing and truly 'Zen' is that?"

In this case history by Glen McDaniel, you'll notice the core foundation is an expectation of good things, with a corollary belief that no hard work is required. When an event the world generally sees as 'bad' takes place, he approaches it with curiosity and openness, knowing that whatever it is, it won't upset his peace of mind.

## *Example #13: Increased Prosperity*

This case study comes from a friend of mine, Mary Kay O'Neil, and it may be easier to include the whole conversation we had, rather than editing it down. This way, you can get a feel for the process of discovering beliefs related to a situation.

**Alan:** What I want to start out with is for you to describe what your situation was before you changed your beliefs about it.

**Mary Kay:** Basically, my situation was that I always felt that I was coming from a place of lack. Even though I managed money well, and I was able to pay my bills and all that kind of thing, I just had this philosophy that I was coming from a place of lack, and when I took the "Keys to the Kingdom" class, we had to sign a contract that we would tithe 10% of our gross income, and that we would tithe 10% of our time, and 10% of our talent.

When I looked at this contract, I thought it was absolutely impossible for me to do that; that I would not have enough money if I did that. I decided that for the seven weeks of the class I would do it but then I would have to quit. So I signed the contract and I just made the commitment to do it, but truly knew that it would be impossible for me to live my life like that.

By the end of the class I was aware, when I wrote my check for the tithe, if I thought the check was big, that meant that I was making a big gross income. So, I saw how much money I had, instead of how much money I was giving away, and I had no problem writing that check and paying all my bills and having enough money left over. So I went from, at the beginning of the seven weeks, a place of lack to the end of the seven weeks, I was coming from a place of abundance.

**Alan:** Let me just break this down just a little bit more for the book. You described what the situation was before you took the class, and as far as the actual process that you went through during the class and making the change: was it more of a change of perspective, a change of perception? Like you said, instead of writing the check and thinking, "Oh, I'm losing money," you're thinking, "Oh, I gained money." At least that's what I'm hearing from what you described.

**Mary Kay:** Right...

**Alan:** Was the process or the action you took between beginning and end, a process of just perception, of mental attitude, or was there some other thing that you did that helped you change that belief?

**Mary Kay:** I think there were a couple of things. One was actually making the commitment. Even though I was only making the commitment for seven weeks at that time. I didn't make the commitment for life, just until the end of the class. Making the commitment seemed to be a piece of it.

And I think I learned a lot of things in the class, especially when I heard other people's stories. I was in a class with people who had been to many of these kinds of classes and had been tithing from their gross for a long, long time. I was the new kid on the block. Hearing their stories reinforced for me that they were doing it.

Another thing that happened kind of coincidentally with this was — my sister is into accounting and she made a budget for me. And even though I always managed my money well, I was always a little bit — I would get the car insurance bill and then I would come up with the money for it; and then I would get a bill for something else and come up with the money for that... and she helped me make a budget where, when my car insurance bill comes in January, there is $400 sitting in that column waiting to be paid. Then I was always ahead of everything. So that was another way for me to put into perspective, on paper, how much I had, instead of concern for what I didn't have.

I think the class really helped me through the process of changing my thinking, but making that commitment for seven weeks, seemed to be the big step.

**Alan:** Ok, so let me just clarify the actual end result of all this. You said that before and after it felt different as far as how you were managing money and how you were able to pay the bills and everything. Did your income actually change during that time, or soon afterwards? Or was the concept of creating a budget enough to make the difference for you?

**Mary Kay:** Boy, my first answer was going to be my income really didn't change, that I just became aware of how much I really had. But I think I want to add to that that I DID have an increase in income. I found out about an annuity that I knew I was going to be getting when I retired from back in the 80's. I found out that I could start collecting it, and then I went through a process of trying to make that happen, which became very complicated. But I did get it and they reimbursed me back to the time I could have started getting it and they even paid me some interest when I requested. I said, "Are you going to pay me interest because it took you so long to give me this?" They even paid me interest. So, that increased my income by $300 a month. And I didn't think I would be getting that until after I was 65. I found out I could get it at 63. So I did have more money coming in subtle, little ways.

So it kind of started out with the same amount of money; I changed my view of it as being — instead of not enough money; I saw it as being a lot of money, and then it changed to other money started dribbling in.

So I had both things.

I could always say before, "I won't be able to tithe because I'm so close to retirement I have to save and have security." I was going to hoard my money for security. And that class changed my mind to, "Let's get it out in circulation."

## *Example #14: Windfall of Money*

This case study comes from Kristen Hartnagel, a singer/songwriter who performs around Michigan and Indiana. What I really like about her story is that it shows how quickly and dramatically you can manifest a desired result simply by setting an intention to do so.

"I was in the car on my way to the Unity Church in Battle Creek, where I was going to be performing, and it was Mother's Day, and I was listening to "The Secret," but I wasn't really conscious of what it was saying. So it was kind of in the background and I recognized that I was thinking my own thoughts.

"And the thoughts I heard myself thinking was, "It's Mother's Day, and nobody's going to be at church, because it's a beautiful day and why would anybody want to spend their time on Mother's Day at church?", especially since a lot of Mothers like to be in the garden or they like to be taken out for a breakfast, and so on.

"In the Catholic Church that I go to, Mother's Day is a big day, where all the kids who never really wanted to go to church would say, "Ok, I'll go to church with you since it's Mother's Day." But that hasn't been my experience in the New Thought Churches.

"And then I heard the part where Jack Canfield from "*Chicken Soup for The Soul*" series had said, "My mentor had told me that I should set a goal so big that I would know that by it coming true that it would be just from what we've been talking about. And you'd have no doubt that the only reason this came true is because you'd been really working on what it is we've been talking about."

"And so I said, "Well, I want to be intentional about today, and today IS Mother's Day, so everybody's going to want to start their day at church. And I'm going to say the right words that are going to reach the right people. I'm going to pick perfect songs." And along with thinking there wasn't going to be a lot of people there was the thought, "I'm driving all this way and I'm probably won't make any money."

"So I said, "Ok, there's going to be more people there than I've ever seen, and I'm going to make more money than I've ever made there before. And the most I've ever made there is $200, so wouldn't it be cool if I made $300. That would tell me that it's just because I'm setting into motion the universe to go before me and organize things just in the way I've imagined; just because it's bigger than I've ever thought, and I'm excited about it." And it was the feeling of, "I can do this. Of course I believe this. I can do this, but I just don't practice it very often."

"And when I got there, there were more people than had ever been there, and I actually made $500. It was really cool. It was like WOW! Why don't I do this all the time?

"It's just that it's the intention and it's the feeling place — because I can think all those positive affirmations in a cerebral way, but when I FEEL it, when I FEEL this is possible, I can do this. This is what creating is about, is getting in that energy of it already being manifested. That's what really brings it around for me."

## *Example #15: The Perfect Vehicle*

Kristen Hartnagel's sister, Lauren Lane Powell, is also a singer/songwriter from Indiana with many wonderful stories about her cross-country travels and how she has used the power of belief to manifest desired outcomes. Together, the two sisters run a website at www.SingForYourSoul.com.

**Lauren**: Well, I think the story I'd love to share is about my new van. It is definitely the most recent, and I started the process of trying to manifest the new vehicle last year, knowing that all of my finances were going into fixing up my old one, which included 2 engines.

**Alan**: Oh Wow!

**Lauren**: Yes… and had I known it was as wonderful and as easy as it was, I probably would have done it before my third engine, but I was still under the belief that I had to make payments, and financing, and come up with a big down payment and all that stuff. So, part of my own issues have been letting go of everything I know that needed to happen that obviously did not need to happen for me to manifest this.

So in June, I had been told by my mechanic that the van I had — the 94 Chevy Astro Van with all my wonderful bumper stickers on it — would probably make it for another year or so, because it had a third engine in it and all the stuff he had done on it. And I think somehow, energetically, my van must have heard that and said "No Way!"

When I was up in Maine, in June or July, it broke down 3 times for 3 different reasons and 3 mechanics later to the tune of about $500 each; I was wondering what the heck was going on. And I knew that because it obviously was not going to make it for another year, it was still costing me money, I was ready for something new, and all of this fear kept coming up. And I finally was able to sit with it in a meditation, and as I prayed, what kept coming up to me was "Why am I afraid?", "What is there to be afraid about getting a new vehicle?" And what came to me was that I was so attached to my old vehicle being 8 years full-time on the road, it was my home away from home.

**Alan**: In other words, it had a lot of good memories attached to it.

**Lauren**: A lot of good memories, and it served me so well. And the feeling of shame started coming up that I was not aware of that I still had. And in that meditation I asked, "What is there to be ashamed of?" And it felt as if I could not look for something better and love what I had at the same time. And it just broke my heart. How can I want something more and love this one at the same time. Was this coming up for me to heal?

And part of my own private work that I am now sharing with the world is what I call a primal purge. And for me, it's going in and asking those very deep questions, like "Where did this come from?", "Where did the feeling of 'I can't love one thing and expect something better at the same time'..." — where did that come from?

And in that meditation I became 3 years old. I remembered a time when I had lost a favored stuffed animal, and it was replaced immediately by a bigger and better stuffed animal and then stuffed animal number 1 was rediscovered. And at 3 years old I learned that I did not have enough love for both. And that's where that duality of "I can't love 2 things at once" came from.

**Alan**: Ok... I was kind of wondering where that was going, and you answered it perfectly.

**Lauren**: It was very painful, but obviously something at that particular moment in time I was ready to see and release.  And so, with this tool that I have kind of rediscovered, I had to hate that stupid, little 3-year-old for believing the untruth.

Now I know that that's not right with my mind, but in my heart and in my gut I was literally going through those feelings that I was not able to express at that age and hate that 3-year-old for deciding that she didn't have enough love.  "And why did you even believe that you couldn't love both of them at the same time.  How stupid can you be?"  And all that trust that I know again was my intellect is not the case.  But I was having to go through the feelings that I was not able to express at 3.

And then obviously the next step was then to forgive that 3-year-old.  Well, at that moment I got out of that meditation, I got a phone call from a friend of mine in Richmond, Virginia, a very wise teacher of mine who's a minister, and he asked pointedly, "How is your van search going?"  I thought, "What in the hell made you ask that at this particular time?  This is so weird."  So, I just shared with him that little story, and he said, "Honey, do you think you have to replace your van?"  And I said, "Well, yeah, that's what's so painful; that's what hurts."  And he said, "Honey, you're not replacing her, you are...," how'd he say it, "... you're validating her.  You're letting her rest.  You are retiring her."  And all of a sudden, that was when I felt that wonderful holy shift.  And I thought, "Yea, I don't have to let her go, I don't have to dislike her in order to find something else.  I'm honoring her, I'm letting her go."

And with that loving energy, Alan, the strangest things started to happen.  My van never was truly fixed after one mechanic after another, but it never did break down again.  And every time I felt it shudder on the road, I started telling it I love it, and how thankful I am that it served me so well, and how I'm looking forward to when I'm letting it rest, and it never gave me an ounce of trouble.

**Alan**:   Yeah, I've had similar experiences with vehicles, too.   It's like, when you're angry with it, or upset with it, or frustrated with it, it knows.

**Lauren**:   Absolutely, absolutely.... Well, and my husband, who's a mechanic-type person; I asked him — I thought he was going to think I was wacko — but I asked him, "Have you ever noticed how your emotions help, or not, your vehicle or your machinery?"   He said, "You know, come to think of it, I've noticed that when men or women hate to mow the lawn, they always have problems with their lawn mower.   And those of us who treat it as a meditation and an opportunity to get outside and be with nature, we rarely have problems with our machinery, and you know, I think there's a lot to be said for that."   I said, "Wow!  What a validation."

So with that love for my new van, I set my sights on something completely better, different than I had ever anticipated coming in, because I knew the result of letting go of those toxic emotions is an opening and a greater awareness for the good that I already have to flow in.   And I know from my own experience, those very toxic emotions are THE blockages to my good.   So the more I can purge and release of those, the more things flow.   So I was really looking forward to something even better and bigger coming into my life.

And in December of 2007, that's what happened.

And in — I don't know if this is even pertinent to the story — but in October, my step son, Phil's son, got into a very bad car accident and, because of prayer, healed so substantially that Phil was able to go out to Oregon and spend a couple of weeks with him, and so ... my husband is a home body, not wanting to go away from home like I do very often.   So, when he came back with his son who was healed so substantially by Christmas time it was absolutely miraculous.

Dylan needed to go up to South Bend, which is about four hours from our house. And Phil was more than willing to leave home again to take him up to South Bend. I said, "Honey, you just got home. You're used to being home, I'm used to being on the road. Let me take him home." So, I drove him up to South Bend, and on my way back, I saw a van, a full-size van, sitting in a parking lot across the street from where I was, that had doors on the driver's side.

Now, I had been putting out there for the last year that I wanted a full-sized vehicle, high top, with doors on the driver's side, but I had yet to see one. Minivans all over the place, doors on both sides, but not full size. Well, when I saw that full-size van with doors on the driver's side, I had just about given up on it, thinking, "Maybe I'm affirming too much. Maybe it just doesn't exist yet." And then when I saw it I said, "Yes, that's what I want, That's exactly what I want. Thank you, God. I know they're in existence, I know it's possible."

Well, less than 5 minutes go by, Alan, and my husband calls. And he said, and I quote, "Have you ever seen a full-size van with doors on the driver's side?" I said, "You're kidding, right? I had it in my brain less than 5 minutes ago, why?" And he said, "I think I found your van on eBay." Because I had done him a favor by taking Dylan up north, he had gotten on eBay specifically to look for my van. And it was in Richmond, VA.

By the time I got home, we were bidding on it, and it didn't meet the amount that the guy wanted. I didn't know if this was even kosher, but I called him. I called him right away, and I said, "I want that vehicle, what is your asking price? How do I do this off of eBay?" And it was so smooth and so easy. It was a 2003 with 48,000 miles, and he was letting it go for $15,000. Now, a couple months later, I found that exact same vehicle for $23,000 in Florida. It was as if God had put that in my face to see what a good deal I really got.

So Phil and I flew out to Richmond, VA right after Christmas, as our Christmas present to each other. We spent the night, met up with some friends, and drove my new vehicle home for the very first time. And it far exceeded any of my expectations with a top-notch radio, not only doors on both sides, but it's a high top, it had a television in it. I mean, it is just so far beyond any kind of opulence in a vehicle that I ever would have thought. And I qualified for an e-loan so quickly it made my head spin. I never did even need my down payment. It was just miraculous!

Well, I think because of this, my husband was really getting in the mood of manifestation himself. Two months later, he was aware that his Nissan Pathfinder — because it was up in Indiana, the underpinning had rusted. The whole body of it is fine, and he was just really bummed because he can't drive it. It's not safe. And he just put out there to the Universe, "You know, I really like this Nissan. I would really like to find something else. I don't even know what." And the next day in the newspaper there was an ad for an Infinity five miles away from us. My husband said, "What's an Infinity? I don't even know what an Infinity is?" Looked it up on the Internet, and "My God, it's a Nissan. My God, it's a Pathfinder. Oh my God, it's the highest end." And he went out and got that for $5,000.

**Alan**: Wow!

**Lauren**: So he is driving a high end, opulent, leather seats, sunroof, Bose stereo and it already had an XM system in there like the Sirius radio I have, that came with it. So, he manifested a vehicle that is so far beyond what he ever imagined himself driving two months after he helped me manifest mine. Oh, and it's so incredible!

So I know that, for me, I need to get rid of anything that is no longer serving me, especially those feelings of undeserving-ness. And as I purge and get rid of all that internal, old, toxic crap, I am literally opening the doors for more and more to flow in. And I tell ya, if the payoff weren't this big, I don't know that I would go through that icky stuff as often as I need to. But that seems to be my path, and that seems to be what works for me.

**Alan**: Definitely a great story. Just to clarify things for myself and for the book — a lot of what you're talking about is changing how you feel about a situation, and I guess what I want to verify with you is that those feelings are based on beliefs, right?

**Lauren**: Yes, and most times, Alan, what I'm learning is that they are core beliefs. They are core beliefs that are formed at a very young age, that maybe did serve me well. I mean, I know that some of my beliefs about my poverty when I was growing up — the judging of those who were wealthy; and having to accept my lot in life, so to speak, of being impoverished — probably saved my butt back then. At least kept me from being grossly unhappy.

But now it's those same beliefs, those same ideas, those same thoughts that are the very things that are getting in my way.

**Alan**: Ok, one other clarification here — you're talking about core beliefs, and I guess I want to check with you as far as how do you define the difference between a core belief and another type of belief.

**Lauren**: Good point. When I was, maybe in my teens, and I saw a movie like "Billy Jack," something that pushed my buttons and brought me home and made me aware of the frailties of life and the injustices, I formed a belief at a very intellectual level that there is injustice in the world, that life isn't fair, and I need to do something to help things be more equal. And that was a belief I think I formed at a very conscious level.

The core beliefs, I believe, are the beliefs that were formed maybe even as early as 8 and under — and I'm just pulling that out of my head because that's another age I formed some really nasty beliefs that are definitely no longer serving me about family. And I think that those are the beliefs that are caused by experience, as children.

And the fact that we don't have the opportunity to verbalize, or to express, the feelings — we hold them in and we don't even realize — it's not conscious at all. I had no idea that I had formed a belief of a dichotomy that there's not enough love to go around. And with that, I believed that I didn't have enough love for those two stuffed animals. Well, how in the world can dad love both Kristen and I at the same level? So all of that just led to one misunderstanding after another, because of that core belief. So I believe that those core beliefs are caused at a very, very young age, that at some level help us make sense, of some kind, of the world that may or may not true.

**Alan**: So you're defining core beliefs more in terms of the age at which you pick them up more so than anything else, although it also sounds like there's an element of whether there's experience involved or not that's also a factor.

**Lauren**: Exactly... exactly.

## *Example #16: Healing of A Relationship*

Our last example comes from another friend of mine, Georgia Monroe, and shows another side to the quirky nature of belief, and how the way you see a situation can completely change your beliefs about it.

**Alan**:  What story would you like to share with the readers of my book?

**Georgia**:  Well actually, it was my relationship with my family and, I guess, my relationship with the world.

**Alan**:  How would you describe those relationships?

**Georgia**:  I did whatever my family told me to do so that, number 1, they would, of course, like me, and number 2, that I wouldn't cause any ripples.  And I guess I kind of did things, kind of safe.

**Alan**:  Ok, so it sounds like you had a belief that you wouldn't be accepted the way you actually were if you just came out and did ....

**Georgia**:  Absolutely, absolutely.

**Alan**:  Ok, so tell me about what you did to change this belief.

**Georgia**:  What I did to change this belief is, I got cancer.  And it made me realize that, number 1, I could die in a year, so I possibly only had one year to look at, and it made me stop and think about what my needs were.  So, when I was diagnosed with cancer, my family wanted to ship me up to my mom's farm, so my mom could take care of me and I would be out of sight, out of mind, ....

**Alan**:  out of the way....

**Georgia**:  Right,  And the bottom line of it was I didn't want to be somewhere else.  If it was my last year, I wanted to be home in my own house with my own things.  And so I just thought, "Well, this is what I really want."  It's the first time I ever really looked at what do I really want.  And so, I kinda told my family, "You know what?  That's not what I want to do.  This is what I want to do.  And if you can't come and take care of me, that's fine, because I have friends that can do that. So I'm not trying to put you on the spot, but this is what I want to do, and this is what I need to do, and this is what I'm going to do."

And, gee, my mom came down and took care of me for six weeks. And my mom was 87, so she wasn't young. And I changed my relationship with my mother. We never had a relationship, and we had a wonderful relationship after that because for six weeks we got true and honest with each other and became our own selves with each other. And I think we both saw in each other some things we had never seen before.

When I got cancer, I looked at it as a gift from the Universe. And there were many gifts I was going to get from it. And one of the gifts was a relationship with my mother because my mom was 87 and she lived to be 93. So I had six really good years of a great relationship with her, which I would have never had if I didn't have cancer.

So, that was just a wonderful gift. And I met many people, and I changed a lot of relationships with a lot of different people because of that. And even today, I am still getting gifts from that. Because a lot of people who their friends or family end up with cancer, call me and ask me if I will touch base with that person and talk to that person or tell them my story. And so I've met all of these people and been a part of their lives. And if I hadn't had cancer, I never would have met them, because nobody would have introduced us because that was kind of the link. So to today, I can say, seven years later, I'm still getting gifts.

So it makes me realize when I get a challenge in my life — I mean it's not that you don't go through the "Oh my God, what am I going to do," and that kind of phase — but when I do get a big challenge, and that's probably the biggest, I think, "Ok, let's look at this differently.

Let's look at this challenge as a gift and see what kind of gifts I can get out of it."

And so, that's kind of what I got out of that.

**Alan**: So, it sounds to me, if I'm going to reinterpret this, is that when you were diagnosed, you were in this place where, "Ok, it's not really going to matter what I do, and if I'm going to do this at all at any point in time, I might as well just do it now."

**Georgia**: If I'm ever going to be me, this is the time.

**Alan**: It sounds like that might have been scary before, but now with the other situation, it didn't seem so scary anymore.

**Georgia**: Absolutely not! It wasn't anywhere near as scary as the cancer was. Yeah! Exactly!

**Alan**: So it was more of a matter of the cancer situation putting the relationship situation in a different perspective.

**Georgia**: Right! right.

**Alan**: And then you stepped out in that direction, probably still a little timid and nervous about it, even though maybe not quite so fearful, and because of the way it went, it went better than you expected it to go? Would that be a fair assessment?

**Georgia**: No..... To be honest with you, I wasn't even timid about it. I was, just, "You know what, this is my needs and this is my wants, and I'm 53 years old and it's about time that I stepped up to the plate" kind of thing. And so I wasn't timid about it, and I was just, for some reason, I just became real.

# Chapter 8:  Helping Others

N ow that you've learned how to improve your own life using the power of belief, it's a natural step to want to help others improve their lives as well.  And since most of us believe that "what goes around, comes around," we will actually benefit ourselves when we go out of our way to help others.

Of course, karma isn't the only reason to help other people. If you've ever been on a diet, you know it's a lot easier to lose weight when those closest to you are following the same diet plan. It's hard to stick to a diet when you're constantly surrounded by folks stuffing their faces with all sorts of junk food.

The same is true when you're on a mental diet and ridding yourself of old limiting beliefs.  It's a lot easier when those around you are also following the same mental diet and not tempting you to believe in limitation and failure.  Many successful people refuse to watch TV news programs for exactly this reason.

There's also a third reason to involve other people in your quest for a better life.  Others can usually see our limiting beliefs better than we can ourselves, and when groups get together to work with this material, everyone benefits.  Not only can the group members help each other find the hidden beliefs stopping us from experiencing the fullness of joy we desire, but the group also acts as a support system to give us encouragement and motivation to keep at it until we succeed.

I know that for myself and many others, having a group to report to once a week is strong motivation to invest the time and effort required to make this material productive.  If left to ourselves, many of us would put it off forever and never get around to putting this information to practical use.  With a group supporting you, it's "put up or shut up."

## *"Choose To Believe" MasterMind Groups*

When you first invite a group of friends and colleagues together to study and practice this material, you may want to follow a proven format. This allows you to start in a comfortable environment. As your group becomes more acquainted with the principles and how they are applied in individual situations, you may find your own way of working together.

Most successful MasterMind groups begin with a brief period where everyone reports on the progress they've made over the previous week. Many groups like to start the session with a prayer or short meditation, and this is fine. When this is done, results are reported right after the opening prayer or meditation.

In the beginning, these progress reports usually reflect the way each person feels about the issues they are working on, and they may not have actual physical results to report. This is fine and a good indication of early progress. As time goes on, there will be actual physical events and experiences to report, and these will help new members realize the possibilities awaiting them.

Regardless of whether results are subjective (feelings only) or objective (actual physical results), all members should be called upon to report, and all results should be complimented and supported by everyone in the group. This is very important, and is one of the primary reasons for having a MasterMind group.

After each member reports their results, each person offers information or inspiration to the group. This may be a section from this book, another book, or it may be an article about someone who has successfully used the power of belief to create change in their life. Since most groups like to keep their meetings shorter than two hours, each person with information to share should keep their portion to ten minutes or less.

After this sharing of new information, successful MasterMind groups will turn their attention to helping each member with whatever challenges they may be facing. This may be in finding hidden beliefs, finding new beliefs to replace them with, presenting possibilities to use in creative daydreaming or creative pretending, or suggestions for physical action that may lead to the desired goal.

This section of the meeting can be thought of as "group coaching" or brainstorming, where each member of the group receives help and advice on how to proceed towards their goal. As with the information sharing phase, this time should be kept short, maybe between 10 and 15 minutes per member. The idea is to present ideas to work with, not solve the issue at hand.

Groups starting their sessions with an opening prayer will usually close with another prayer. Other ways of ending a MasterMind group session would be to state an intention for the following week, or to have each member commit to a certain level of activity, such as a number of belief conditioning sessions or one or more practical steps towards their goals.

Another aspect of successful MasterMind groups is that they all have a set of "ground rules" that are in effect during their meetings, such as "no criticism is allowed without a corresponding suggestion for improvement" or "no one is allowed to speak for more than 10 minutes at a time." Many sample sets of rules may be found online. Feel free to use one of them or make up your own rules.

The general guideline is to simply be courteous, kind, and supportive. Each member should feel they are supported and a vital part of the group, and any behavior counterproductive to this goal should not be allowed.

One final thought on MasterMind groups is that many people feel they should be relatively small — ten members or less. This allows everyone to have enough time to share with the group within a reasonably short meeting.

## *Reaching Out*

Having a MasterMind group is an excellent way to help others while also helping yourself, however, there will also be times when you feel a need to help another person alter their beliefs about an issue outside the group.

This may happen because this person is a friend and you want to see your friend happy and satisfied. Or this person may be someone you have to work with on an ongoing basis, and you don't want to have to deal with their negative beliefs every day. Maybe this person is in a position of authority over you, and you need them to believe in you and what you can do.

One thing you could do is loan them a copy of this book so they understand the importance of choosing their own beliefs. However, this isn't always appropriate, so in many cases you'll want to use a gentle form of persuasion to lead them to a better outlook. We talked about just such a thing in Chapter 5. It's called conversational hypnosis.

Conversational hypnosis isn't about getting people to close their eyes and count backwards from 100 to 1. It's also not about conning others to give up the things they want or to buy something they don't need. Conversational hypnosis was created by psychologists to help people believe in a better way of approaching life, and has been instrumental in creating personal change in dramatic ways. We discussed this briefly in Chapter 5.

In fact, Anthony Robbins uses a form of conversational hypnosis in his Personal Power courses and seminars, which have helped thousands of people become more effective individuals and lead happier lives.

Over the next few pages, I will share with you some of the most powerful aspects of conversational hypnosis. As you develop these skills, your relationships with other people will quickly grow more harmonious and enjoyable, and you'll notice it's easier to get the things you want in life. In fact, you may find yourself wanting to learn more, at which point I will direct you to check out my *"Keys To Power Persuasion"* course at www.KeysToPowerPersuasion.com.

## *Pink Elephant Principle*

The first principle of conversational hypnosis states the human mind has an automatic nature. To understand what another person says, either verbally or in writing, your mind must interpret the words used into their mental equivalents.

For instance, when we read the section heading above, most of us will have an image of a pink elephant running through our minds. If I were to talk to you about a dog, you will most likely have an image pop up in your mind. And if I were to talk about love, you may notice a warm feeling well up within you.

There are several ways this principle can be used to help alter another person's beliefs. The first is through story-telling. When you tell a story about how someone faced their fears and came out okay, you give your listener a vicarious experience supporting a belief that it's okay to face their fears. And if you tell a story about someone who suddenly became very successful after a lifetime of toil and frustration, you help your listener to believe it's possible for them to succeed quickly as well, despite past experiences. Of course, the best stories are those that are based in fact, although even fiction stories work well for this.

A great example of this is the woman who wanted her husband to treat her with kindness and respect instead of demanding she obey his wishes all the time. One night, she told him story after story about other men (presumably friends of hers) who had found that treating their wives with kindness and respect led to them getting more of what they wanted from the relationship. After several such stories, and no other promptings, this woman noticed her husband being more attentive and respectful during the following week. A short time later, she told her husband another group of stories about men who had found a new sense of pride in their ability to keep their wives happy, even with no expectation of reward or compensation. Soon afterwards, she noticed he seemed to be trying to outdo himself to please her in every way he could.  When he was asked why he was doing all this, his response was, "It makes me feel good to see her happy."

Another way of using the Pink Elephant Principle is with a concept called 'linking'.  You may remember from Chapter 5 how the human mind naturally associates things together as part of the learning process.  You may also remember that, for our purposes, we link the feeling of trust and confidence to what we want to believe, or in this case, what we want our listener to believe.

For example, if you need someone to trust you, you can use this principle to elicit a feeling of trust within your listener.  You do this by talking about trust, about people who are trustworthy, and about situations where trust is expected.  Immediately after eliciting a feeling of trust, you bring yourself into the conversation, and even though you may not actually come out and say "trust me," your listener will automatically link the feeling of trust to you, and they will naturally trust you more than they did before.

Advertisers use the concept of linking all the time.  Everywhere you look, you'll see ads that evoke a feeling of confidence, fun, excitement, or safety while promoting a product or service.  Many ads will evoke a feeling of pain or fear, but only as a contrast to the benefits of buying the product advertised.  (Do you remember us talking about the contrast principle in Chapter 5?  This is one way it's used.)

## *Pacing and Leading Statements*

In Chapter 5, we talked about how the concept of pacing and leading may be used to help boost our level of belief in whatever we wish.  As mentioned there, this concept was originally developed to persuade other people to accept new beliefs.

By pacing your listener with a series of statements they feel are obviously true; such as where you are, what you're doing, and how you're doing it; a feeling of trust and believability is elicited.  When you bring up an idea that may not be obviously true, the feeling of trust is automatically transferred (or linked) to the new idea. As long as your listener doesn't feel this new idea is "obviously false," they will believe the new idea more than they did a few minutes ago.

Here's an example of this being used in real life:

> "Thanks for agreeing to see me today. I know you're a busy man and you have a lot of responsibility. I also know you don't like to waste time and you want to make sure that whatever we do in this case is right. I want to do my part to make sure everything goes well."

In this example, the speaker makes four pacing statements and finishes with one leading statement. If the listener had been concerned that the speaker may have been out for his or her own interests, this will help ease those concerns. In actual use, this group of statements would be used as a lead-in to the speaker's ideas for how to proceed, or maybe some questions to elicit more information from the listener.

As in our belief work, each set of pacing and leading statements will shift your listener's beliefs by a small amount, and significant change takes place when you string together a longer series of such groups. You'll also notice you get better results when you use the suggestions from Chapter 6 and work from general to specific, taking small steps to reach your goal. Even so, you'll be amazed how much you can alter your listener's beliefs in a short period of time.

## *Embedded Commands*

For many, the whole point of using any type of hypnosis is to deliver commands that will be acted upon by the listener's subconscious mind. When the person you want to influence is awake and alert, these commands need to be subliminal in nature and not consciously recognized. In conversational hypnosis, these take the form of command statements embedded within a larger sentence.

For example:

> "I certainly wouldn't dream of asking you to **stop what you're doing**, and you're free to **cooperate with me** or not, but wouldn't it be great if we could find a way to **work together** while we ponder what we have here?"

When the above sentence is spoken, the embedded commands (the parts in **bold**) are spoken with slightly more intensity, with a very brief pause before and afterwards. Although the difference goes unnoticed on a conscious level, the effect is unmistakable and often immediate. Within moments, you can gain someone's cooperation when they were previously focused on doing their own thing.

It's important to remember that embedded commands need to be delivered with a *subtle* difference from the rest of your communication. If your listener notices what you're doing, then the process self-destructs and works against you.

Here's another example of embedded commands:

> "I know it must seem that the world is against you right now, and it may be difficult to **consider the world your friend**, but sooner or later, you'll find **things will get better** and you'll **be happy for what you have now**."

When you have a friend who is seriously frustrated or depressed, the best thing you can do is give them hope. In many cases, I've found that coming right out and telling them that things will get better is usually ineffective, yet subtly suggesting happier possibilities brings quick results.

> "I completely understand your pain. I've had times
> where I didn't want to think about how **things could
> be better**, or to **imagine bright sunny days**,
> especially when it seemed everything was against
> me. However, as true as the sky is blue, no matter
> how hard I tried to stay angry, **the anger slips away**
> and leaves an empty space to start over again."

This example combines the use of embedded commands with
the Pink Elephant Principle to help the listener release their anger
and get ready to move forward with hopefulness. There are other
principles involved, such as associative linking and a suggestion
that the anger will slip away despite any effort to keep it.

Embedded commands are usually short and simple phrases;
such as "feel better," "believe in success," or "respect me"; fitting
neatly into practically any sentence structure. However, as in the
last example above, embedded commands may also be used to
help your listener focus on some aspects of what you're saying
more than other parts.

Another aspect of embedded commands is that they can be
used more directly when you're telling a story. Good storytellers
will usually quote dialog said by the characters in the story, such
as:

> "Mary looked right at Jack and said, '**I wouldn't go
> out with you if you were the last man on Earth.
> You need a shave, it's been days since you've
> taken a bath, and your clothes are all dirty.**' and
> then immediately turned and walked out the door."

This example (which presumably is part of a longer story)
would be good if you needed to subtly suggest to someone they
need to take better care of their hygiene without having to
confront them about it.

The good thing about using stories is that you have a level of indirection between the messages in the story and the person you're talking to. If someone were to ask, "Are you referring to me in that story?", you can always reply, "No, of course not!" That way, the message gets across without you looking like the villain.

## *Faith Anchoring*

Between the Pink Elephant Principle, pacing and leading, and embedded commands, you have a powerful set of tools to elicit any feeling you want your listener to experience, especially the feelings of trust and confidence we use to alter beliefs. With the use of anchors, you can set up an automatic response in your listener so you can call those feelings forth any time you wish without having to elicit them all over again.

Anchors are formed when our minds associate a feeling with an action, such as a touch on a shoulder, an expression on someone's face, or even a tone of voice when they speak a particular word. You can direct your listener to form an anchor between the feeling of trust and a particular gesture simply by making that gesture any time you talk about trust.

Once an anchor is formed, you apply it any time you want your listener to associate the feeling linked to that anchor with what you're talking about at the time.

For example, let's say that over a period of time (minutes, hours, or days), you've spoken frequently about trust to a particular person, and each time you've made a slight gesture that does not call attention to itself, such as touching your thumb to your third finger, or placing your hand near your heart. Over this time, not only has this person learned to associate this gesture with trust, but has also grown to trust you more since the issue has come up a number of times.

Now, you want to introduce a new concept to this person, such as taking more time to do higher-quality work, or maybe becoming more interested in the people around him or her. This person may have resisted this idea in the past, but as you bring it up again while making the trust gesture, there is a subconscious nudging that gently pushes him or her to consider the idea more trustworthy.

Of course, if you also apply some of the other conversational techniques, such as embedded commands, pacing and leading statements, and the Pink Elephant Principle (to make the concept more palatable), this person will find themselves thinking about the idea in a new light.

You don't always have to create anchors in the people you work with. If you notice they respond to a particular gesture, touch, or word with the response you want, you can use the pre-existing anchor just as easily as you can use one you create yourself.

## Using Other Techniques

Any of the techniques we discussed in Chapter 5 may be used in our conversations with other people to help them alter their beliefs. Belief leverage is perhaps one of the most common ways people influence each other. Whenever we refer to a concept our listener already believes, this acts like a placebo to create change.

Those who believe in a God who answers prayers will be influenced when you tell them you've been praying for their recovery. Those who believe in energy therapies will be influenced when you go through the motions associated with their particular belief system. And those who believe in statistics will be influenced when you talk about the statistics proving that those who do business online make more money with less effort than with any other business structure.

There's one catch, however. The person you're trying to influence has to *believe* that what you're saying or doing is genuine. If you offer to perform an energy therapy to help them recover from a surgery, it won't do anything if they don't believe you've been properly 'trained' for that therapy. And all the statistics in the world won't persuade a person who doesn't believe the sources are trustworthy.

Also keep in mind that beliefs are based on the person's overall experience in a particular area, and the depth at which new information is learned. If the person you want to help has had a thousand experiences of failure, it will take more than one or two casual suggestions to help them believe in success. On the other hand, if you have their full cooperation and use the techniques taught in this book, you can help them see much quicker results.

And there's nothing more satisfying than realizing you have the power to help other people enjoy lives of harmonious and joyful anticipation for the future.

# Now What?

We've covered a great deal of territory in this book. We've looked at the scientific evidence supporting the concept that our beliefs create our reality. We've also covered what you can do to determine which beliefs may be obstructing you from your goals, and what you can do to change them. We've even covered a variety of useful guidelines to help you utilize this information effectively and efficiently.

If you're like me, you've read through this book without doing the exercises or attempting to make any changes to your beliefs. That's okay. I do this because I want to understand the overall picture first before getting involved in the details. If this describes you as well, then now is the time to *go through this book again*, this time implementing the ideas and suggestions.

One thing I can say from my own personal experience — it doesn't matter how much you read, you'll NEVER get a complete understanding of this field until you have direct, personal experience working with it. It's like being trained for a new job, you really don't know what questions to ask until you've been working a while.

You'll also find that working with others in a group situation will make the whole process much easier to understand and implement. Check to see if anyone has already started a MasterMind group in your area, and if not, start one yourself. This will give you extra support and motivation to put the information into practice.

Depending on your goals and your needs, you may also want to consider sponsoring a *Choose To Believe* workshop in your area. Contact me at www.PowerKeysPub.com/contact for details.

However you proceed, I'd love to hear about your experiences as you put these ideas into practice.

# Bibliography

Books are wonderful sources of information and inspiration. What follows is a list of books in my own personal library. Some are scholarly scientific texts, whereas others are examples of the fun we can have with beliefs. They have helped me in many ways. May they serve you as well as they have served me.

Achterberg, Jeanne. *"Imagery in Healing: Shamanism and Modern Medicine."* Shambhala Publications, 1985

Anderson, U.S. *"Three Magic Words."* Wilshire Book Company, 1954

Atkinson, William Walker. *"Mind-Power: The Secret of Mental Magic."* Yogi Publication Society, 1912, 1940

Bach, Marcus. *"The Will to Believe."* Prentice-Hall, 1955

Bandler, Richard, John Grinder. *"The Structure of Magic – Vol. I."* Science and Behavior Books, 1975

Bandler, Richard, John Grinder. *"The Structure of Magic – Vol. II."* Science and Behavior Books, 1976

Barnstone, Willis, ed. *"The Other Bible."* Harper & Row, 1984

Bernd, Ed. *"José Silva's Ultramind ESP System."* New Page Books, 2000

Blair, Forbes Robbins. *"Instant Self-Hypnosis."* SourceBooks, 2004

Blaze, Chrissie and Gary. *"Power Prayer."* Adams Media, 2004

Bohm, David. *"Wholeness and the Implicate Order."* Routledge, 1980

Braden, Gregg. *"The Divine Matrix: Bridging Time, Space, Miracles, and Belief."* Hay House, 2007

Bristol, Claude M. *"The Magic of Believing."* Simon & Schuster, 1948

Bristol, Claude, Harold Sherman. *"TNT: The Power Within You."* Prentice-Hall, 1954

Butterworth, Eric. *"Spiritual Economics."* Unity Books, 1983, 1998

Cialdini, Robert B. *"Influence: Science and Practice."* Allyn and Bacon, 2001

Cunningham, Scott. *"Hawaiian Religion & Magic."* Llewellyn Publications, 1994

Denning, Melita, Osborne Phillips. *"The Llewellyn Practical Guide to Creative Visualization."* Llewellyn Publications, 1983, 1987

Diaz, Al. *"The Titus Concept: Money for My Best and Highest Good."* Morgan James Publishing, 2005

Dodd, Ray. *"The Power of Belief."* Hampton Roads Publishing Company, 2003

Dodd, Ray. *"BeliefWorks."* Hampton Roads Publishing Company, 2006

Dyer, Wayne. *"Your Erroneous Zones."* Avon Books, 1976

Dyer, Wayne. *"You'll See It When You Believe It."* Avon Books, 1989

Dyer, Wayne. *"Real Magic."* HarperCollins, 1992

Dyer, Wayne. *"The Power of Intention."* Hay House, 2004

Erickson, Milton, Ernest Rossi. *"Hypnotherapy: An Exploratory Casebook."* Irvington Publishers, 1979

Filmore, Charles. *"Christian Healing."* Unity Books, 1909

Filmore, Charles. *"Prosperity."* Unity Books, 1936

Finley, Guy. *"The Secret of Letting Go."* Llewellyn Publications, 2007

Fort, Charles. *"The Complete Books of Charles Fort."* Dover Publications, 1974

Frank, Jerome D. *"Persuasion and Healing."* The John Hopkins Press, 1961

Frost, Charles. *"The Possible You."* Blue Dolphin Publishing, 1999

Gawain, Shakti. *"Living in the Light."* New World Library, 1986

Gill, Merton, Margaret Brenman. *"Hypnosis and Related States."* International Universities Press, 1959

Godwin, John. *"Super-Psychic: The Incredible Dr. Hoy."* Pocket Books, 1974, 1977

Haisch, Bernard. *"The God Theory."* WeiserBooks, 2006

Haraldsson, Erlendur. *"Modern Miracles."* Hastings House, 1987, 1997

Hewitt, William W. *"Hypnosis for Beginners."* Llewellyn Publications, 1986, 1987, 1997

Hicks, Esther & Jerry. *"The Amazing Power of Deliberate Intent."* Hay House, 2006

Hogan, Kevin, James Speakman. *"Covert Persuasion."* John Wiley & Sons, 2006

Holmes, Ernest. *"The Science of Mind."* G. P. Putnam's Sons, 1938, 1966, 1988

Holmes, Ernest. *"How to Change Your Life."* Health Communication, Inc., 1982, 1999

Kiev, Ari, ed. *"Magic, Faith, and Healing."* The Free Press of Glencoe, 1964

Laurence, Theodor, ed. *"The Parker Lifetime Treasury of Mystic and Occult Powers."* Reward Books, 1978

LeCron, Leslie M, ed. *"Experimental Hypnosis."* The Citadel Press, 1968

Lipton, Bruce. *"The Biology of Belief."* Mountain of Love Productions, 2005

Long, Max Freedom. *"The Secret Science Behind Miracles."* DeVorss & Company, 1948, 1976

Long, Max Freedom. *"Growing Into Light."* DeVorss & Company, 1955

Long, Max Freedom. *"What Jesus Taught in Secret."* DeVorss & Company, 1983

Mahoney, Michael J. *"Human Change Processes: The Scientific Foundations of Psychotherapy."* BasicBooks, 1991

Maltz, Maxwell. *"Psycho-Cybernetics."* Prentice-Hall, 1960

Maltz, Maxwell. *"Creative Living for Today."* Essandess Special Editions, 1967

Manning, Al G. *"Helping Yourself with ESP."* Reward Books, 2000

McKay, Matthew, Patrick Fanning. *"Change Your Mind, Change Your Life."* MJF Books, 1991

Millman, Dan. *"Everyday Enlightenment."* Warner Books, 1998

Moine, Donald, Kenneth Lloyd. *"Unlimited Selling Power."* Prentice Hall, 1990

Murphy, Joseph. *"Special Meditations for Health, Wealth, Love, and Expression."* DeVorss & Company, 1952, 1980

Murphy, Joseph. *"Quiet Moments with God."* DeVorss & Company, 1958

Murphy, Joseph. *"The Power of Your Subconscious Mind."* Reward Books, 1963, 2000

Murphy, Joseph. *"The Miracle of Mind Dynamics."* Reward Books, 1964

Murphy, Joseph. *"Amazing Laws of Cosmic Mind Power."* Reward Books, 1965, 2001

Murphy, Joseph. *"Your Infinite Power to be Rich."* Reward Books, 1966

Murphy, Joseph. *"The Cosmic Power Within You."* DeVorss & Company, 1968, 2002

Murphy, Joseph. *"Psychic Perception."* DeVorss & Company, 1971, 1995

Murphy, Joseph. *"Miracle Power for Infinite Riches."* Reward Books, 1972

Murphy, Joseph. *"Telepsychics."* DeVorss & Company, 1973

Murphy, Joseph. *"The Cosmic Energizer."* DeVorss & Company, 1974, 1995

Murphy, Joseph. *"Within You is the Power."* DeVorss & Company, 1977

Murphy, Joseph. *"How to Use the Laws of Mind."* DeVorss & Company, 1980

Murphy, Joseph. *"Think Yourself Rich."* Reward Books, 2001

O'Connor, Joseph, John Seymour. *"Introducing NLP."* Thorsons, 1990

Ouspensky, P.D. *"Tertium Organum: A Key to the Enigmas of the World."* Vintage Books, 1920, 1922, 1950

Ouspensky, P.D. *"A New Model of the Universe."* Dover Publications, 1931, 1997

Paulina, Anet. *"Transcend the Aging Process."* iUniverse, 2004

Ponder, Catherine. *"The Dynamic Laws of Prosperity."* DeVorss & Company, 1962, 1985

Ponder, Catherine. *"Dare to Prosper."* DeVorss & Company, 1983

Ponder, Catherine. *"The Dynamic Laws of Prayer."* DeVorss & Company, 1987

Radin, Dean. *"The Conscious Universe: The Scientific Truth of Psychic Phenomena."* HarperEdge, 1997

Ray, James Arthur. *"The Science of Success."* SunArk Press, 2006

Rhine, Louisa E. *"Mind Over Matter."* Collier Books, 1970, 1972

Robbins, Anthony. *"Unlimited Power."* Free Press, 1986

Roth, Charles. *"Mind: The Master Power."* Unity Books, 1974, 1997

Russell, Bertrand. *"A History of Western Philosophy."* Simon & Schuster, 1945, 1972

Schwartz, Dr. David J. *"The Magic of Thinking Big."* Prentice-Hall, 1959, 1965

Schwartz, Dr. David J. *"The Magic of Thinking Success."* Wilshire Book Company, 1987

Silva, José, Philip Miele. *"The Silva Mind Control Method."* Simon & Schuster, 1977

Sommer, Bobbe. *"Psycho-Cybernetics 2000."* Prentice-Hall, 1993

Stanley, Thomas J. *"The Millionaire Mind."* Andrews McMeel Publishing, 2001

Stelter, Alfred. *"Psi-Healing."* Bantam Books, 1976

Stevens, Jose & Lena. *"Secrets of Shamanism."* Avon Books, 1988

Sudre, René. *"Para-Psychology."* The Citadel Press, 1960

Talbot, Michael. *"The Holographic Universe."* HarperCollins, 1991

Tutt, Alan. *"Keys To Power – Step by Step Course."* PowerKeys
    Publishing, 2003
Tutt, Alan. *"Keys To Power Prosperity."* PowerKeys Publishing,
    2004
Tutt, Alan. *"Keys To Power Persuasion."* PowerKeys Publishing,
    2006
Tyrrell, G.N.M. *"Science and Psychical Phenomena:
    Apparitions."* University Books, 1961
Watson, Lyall. *"Beyond Supernature."* Bantam Books, 1987
Webster, Richard. *"Miracles: Inviting the Extraordinary Into
    Your Life."* Llewellyn Publication, 2004
Weed, Joseph. *"Wisdom of the Mystic Masters."* Reward Books,
    1968
Whitcomb, Bill. *"The Magician's Companion."* Llewellyn
    Publications, 1985, 1993
Yogananda, Paramahansa. *"Autobiography of a Yogi."* Self-
    Realization Fellowship, 1946, 1974
Zondervan NIV Study Bible, 1985, 1995, 2002

## *Other References*

These are not in my personal library, and are here because
they are referenced in Chapters 1 and 4.

DiRita, V. J. *"Genomics Happens"* Science 289:1488-1489, 2000
Klopfer, Bruno. *"Psychological Variables in Human Cancer"*
    Journal of Prospective Techniques, 31:331-340, 1957
Null, G., Ph.D., C. Dean, M.D. N.D., et al. *"Death by Medicine."*
    Nutritional Institute of America, 2003
Starfield, B. *"Is US Health Really the Best in the World?"* Journal
    of the American Medical Association, 284(4):483-485, 2000

# Index

# Also Available From PowerKeys Publishing

## Choose To Believe Essential Package

- *Choose To Believe* ebook
- *28 Days to Effortless Success* ebook
- 2008 Choose To Believe workshop audio recordings
- 2011 Choose To Believe workshop audio recordings

Although the above material presents the same concepts shared in this book, each one presents it in a slightly different way, thereby helping you reach a deeper understanding of the concepts involved.

## Choose To Believe Deluxe Package

Includes the complete Essential Package above, plus:

- Complete Self-Esteem module from *EmBRACES Belief Entrainment System* (36 recordings)
- *Law of Attraction Insider* teleseminar series (23 recordings plus transcripts)
- 5 additional teleseminars featuring Alan Tutt.

The material available in the Deluxe Package extends what you've learned here, and helps you implement it in a variety of ways. The *EmBRACES* Self-Esteem module used to sell for $97 just by itself.

Both of the above packages are fully described at www.PowerKeysPub.com/choose-to-believe. Use the following coupon code during checkout to get an instant 20% discount off the regular price of either package: **IownTheBook**

## EmBRACES* Belief Entrainment System

For those who want maximum results with minimum effort. The *EmBRACES Belief Entrainment System* includes 360 recordings of background audio (120 full CDs worth) which combine BWE, NLP, NSS, and 492 belief statements to condition your mind for true success. Covers all areas, from self-esteem and self-sufficiency, to confidence, motivation, productivity, self-mastery, peace of mind, relationships, and prosperity.

One of the main problems with most mind-conditioning materials is that they repeat a handful of statements over and over again with the same voice and the same music. As such, your inner mind quickly identifies it as a repeating pattern, and tunes it out before it has a chance to produce any results.

With the *EmBRACES Belief Entrainment System*, multiple voices are used, with a wide variety of music and tones to create a highly textured audio experience which remains non-distracting, yet keeps your inner mind engaged and listening. This maximizes the results you get.

Further enhancing your self-development, the belief statements are not subliminal, but are presented in a low-key manner which presents minimal distraction. This "not-so-subliminal" (NSS) approach has been proven to work time and time again.

Each recording in the EmBRACES Essential Package includes a BrainWave Entrainment (BWE) track which gently shifts your brain into a highly relaxed and receptive state, the ideal state for learning new material.

Both of the above packages are fully described at www.PowerKeysPub.com/belief-entrainment.

* – EmBRACES stands for:
Empowering Belief Reinforcement and Alignment for
Confidence, Excellence, and Success.

## *Harmonic Prayer*

Alan Tutt's newest book, *"Harmonic Prayer: How to Instantly Increase Your Prayer Power"* brings the science of NLP (Neuro-Linguistic Programming) to the practice of prayer.

Based on a belief that prayer works best when the conditions of faith, focus, and a feeling of harmony with God are strong, *Harmonic Prayer* explains how to elicit each of these conditions within seconds.

As with most other products available on the PowerKeys Publishing website, there are two packages available.

### *Essential Package*

- *Harmonic Prayer* ebook
- Magic & Miracles mini-module from the *EmBRACES* system (Focus mode — 12 recordings, 4 CDs)
- Focus CD (guided meditations to help you focus)
- Feeling CD (guided meditations to establish a feeling of harmony with God)
- Prayer Session CD (BWE-enhanced background to help you focus during prayer)
- BWE resource CD (BWE sessions to help increase IQ, creativity, and healing, as well as reduce anxiety.

### *Deluxe Package*

All of the above, plus:

- Remaining 8 CDs from *EmBRACES* Magic & Miracles module.
- Complete *EmBRACES* Confidence module (12 CDs)

Both packages are fully described at
www.PowerKeysPub.com/harmonic-prayer.

## Awaken the Avatar Within

Similar to *Harmonic Prayer*, *Awaken the Avatar Within* (due to come out in 2012) presents its material without the religious overtones.

For more information on this book and associated packages, go to www.PowerKeysPub.com/awaken-the-avatar-within.

## Prosperity From the Inside Out

Taking the core ideas from *Choose To Believe* and addressing the issue of prosperity directly, *Prosperity From the Inside Out* starts by addressing the specific beliefs required for abundant prosperity, and then expands by covering a variety of practical tips and tricks for attracting money from every direction.

## Treasure Map to Online Riches

The Internet has been responsible for more "overnight millionaires" than anything else in history. In this 157-page report, Alan Tutt explains the key principles involved in building an online business that is practically guaranteed to be a success.

Covering everything from basic concepts, to step-by-step instructions for setting up a profitable website, to high-end marketing principles previously available only in $2000 course, *Treasure Map to Online Riches* is literally a gold mine of high-value information.

Both of the above books, plus associated packages, may be found at www.PowerKeysPub.com/prosperity.

## PowerKeys Pointers Mailing List

To stay up to date with everything that happens on the PowerKeys Publishing website, including new releases, sign up to our mailing list at www.PowerKeysPub.com/powerkeys-pointers.

## *Quantity Discounts*

Do you have a study group and would like to save money on books?  Or are you planning a fund-raiser and want to feature something new and exciting?  Or does your business need a large quantity of low-priced items to use as sales incentives?

If any of these describe you, PowerKeys Publishing can help with our generous quantity discount program.

For small groups, buy 4 or more books, and get the standard bookstore discount of 40%.  If you buy 20 or more, you get the full wholesale discount of 50%.

Those needing larger quantities can move up to our corporate or distributor levels with discounts of 60% and 70% respectively.  To qualify, your purchase must be 100 or 500 copies of the same book.

Here's a chart to make it easy to figure your discount:

| Minimum # of Copies | Discount off regular price |
|---------------------|----------------------------|
| 4                   | 40%                        |
| 20                  | 50%                        |
| 100                 | 60%                        |
| 500                 | 70%                        |

Quantity discounts are automatically applied when placing orders on the PowerKeys Publishing website.  If you need (or want) any assistance, just use the contact form on the website.  www.PowerKeysPub.com/contact

Lightning Source UK Ltd.
Milton Keynes UK
UKOW05f2035190916

283372UK00012B/197/P